Blacks and Science
Volume Two

Blacks and Science Volume Two

*West and East African
Contributions to
Science and Technology*

AND

*Intellectual Life and Legacy
of Timbuktu*

BY

Robin Walker

REKLAW EDUCATION LTD
London (U.K.)

ISBN-13: 978-1492996231

ISBN-10: 1492996238

Cover design by Robin Walker

CONTENTS

OPENING REMARKS

Ancient West Africa, its history and its achievements, should be of great interest and importance to many people, least of the all the African Diaspora in Britain, the Americas and the Caribbean. Most of this Diaspora are of distant West African origins but many find little pride in this fact. Africa does not get a good press. Moreover, the only countries in Africa that are generally spoken of with admiration or respect for its scientific and intellectual achievements are the North African countries of Egypt and Morocco. West Africa and its achievements are hardly ever spoken of with admiration. On the contrary--West Africa is merely portrayed as the historical hunting ground for people to enslave.

The case of East Africa is somewhat similar. With the exception of Ethiopia, most of East Africa's history and achievements are either unknown to the general public or have been credited to Arabs and Persians rather than to East Africans themselves. Many East Africans continue to believe propaganda put out there by the colonial era governments to the effect that their history is really the history of Arabs and Persians colonising them.

This book, *Blacks and Science Volume Two*, was written to challenge this negativity. I write about what West and East Africans have contributed to scientific, technological and intellectual endeavour. For the record, those achievements amount to rather more than mud huts, calabashes and basket weaving!

In writing this book, I build upon the research of earlier scholars--Professor Cheikh Anta Diop, Professor Ivan Van Sertima, Professor Charles Finch, Mr Hunter Adams, Mr Benaebi Benatari, Professor Rodney Medupe, Professor Otto Neugebauer, Dr A. T. Bryant, Dr Nnamdi Elleh and Professor Claudia Zaslavsky. I bring the information together in an easily accessible and easy to digest way. This is the kind of book that you can share with your children.

This book is largely a synthesis of my previously published Kindle e-books or lecture-essays *West African Contributions to Science and*

Technology combined with *Intellectual Life and Legacy of Timbuktu*. I have added new information not present in either e-book on East Africa.

The feedback I received from these e-books was positive, but many people asked me if was possible to turn these lecture essays into physical books. After all, not everybody possesses a Kindle! My response was to produce this book *Blacks and Science Volume Two*.

The first part of this book is a general introduction to the role played by the West Africans in the evolution of Mathematics, Astronomy & Physics, Metallurgy, Medicine & Surgery, Boat Building & Navigation, Architecture, and Crafts & Industry.

The second part of the book focuses on the intellectual and literary culture of the West African city of Timbuktu. In this section, I discuss the content, importance and implications of the recently rediscovered manuscripts of Timbuktu.

The third part of this book is a general introduction to the role played by the East Africans in the evolution of Mathematics, Architecture, Mining & Metallurgy, Astronomy, Medicine & Surgery, and Shipping & Navigation.

Finally, in the fourth part of the book, I introduce the lectures and courses that I teach on these topic areas.

Read and enjoy

Robin Walker 2015

PART ONE

WEST AFRICAN CONTRIBUTIONS TO SCIENCE AND TECHNOLOGY

PREFACE

When West Africa is mentioned in a historical context, it is usually presented as the traditional hunting ground for slaves. Very few writers have shown any interest in the contributions of West Africans to science and technology. Thus there has been very little research that challenges the perspective that all that West Africans have ever been historically is to be under the whip of other peoples.

Fortunately, the tide is beginning to change, a *National Geographic* article entitled *Reclaiming the Ancient Manuscripts of Timbuktu* mentioned that some scholars believe that 700,000 manuscripts, some dating to the twelfth century, have survived in the West African city of Timbuktu. They also say the manuscripts 'covered an array of subjects: astronomy, medicine, mathematics, chemistry,' etcetera.

The article mentioned other data that is little known today but well worth repeating: 'Beginning in the 12th century, Timbuktu was becoming one of the great centers of learning in the Islamic world. Scholars and students travel[l]ed from as far away as Cairo, Baghdad, and elsewhere in Persia to study from the noted manuscripts found in Timbuktu. Respected scholars who taught in Timbuktu were referred to as ambassadors of peace throughout North Africa.'

Like the *National Geographic* article, this book presents a different side to West African historical achievements. Challenging all stereotypes, it is a general introduction to the exciting role played by early West Africans in the evolution of Mathematics, Astronomy & Physics, Metallurgy, Medicine & Surgery, Boat Building & Navigation, Architecture, and Crafts & Industry.

There are some interesting findings that appear in this text:

o The Bamoun Kingdom, now in today's Cameroon, has 7,000 surviving manuscripts in their own script

o Timbuktu astronomers used the cosine, tangent, cotangent, secant and cosecant functions of trigonometry

o The Dogon of Mali had an early and wholly indigenous notion of 'big bang' derived from a singularity o A number of iron and copper tools were excavated in Senegal that dated from 2800 BC

o The total amount of gold mined in the desert regions of West Africa to the year 1500 was $35 billion at 1998 gold prices

o A surviving sixteenth century Timbuktu manuscript has a formula for making toothpaste and adds that regular brushing of your teeth removes bad breath

o The majority of enslaved Africans were inoculated against smallpox BEFORE they were deported from Africa

o A 1342 text published in Cairo mentions two royal Malian voyages sailing across the Atlantic involving hundreds of vessels

o The Royal Palace of the Ashanti Empire contained a suite of apartments on its upper floor that reminded a visitor to the palace of Wardour Street in Central London

o Glass was manufactured at the Yoruba capital of Ile-Ife in the sixth century AD

Finally:

o According to *New Scientist,* there are even surviving Timbuktu manuscripts that deal with climatology

INTRODUCTION

This part of the book concentrates on the ancient and mediaeval West African contributions to science and technology. The focus is on the West African superstates of Ancient Ghana, Mediaeval Mali, and the Songhai Empire. This essay also looks at the contributions made by the states near to the West African coast including Nok, Igbo-Ukwu, Ife, Benin, Kongo and Ashanti. I have also included evidence from more inland including the Kuba and Shongo cultures located towards Central Africa.

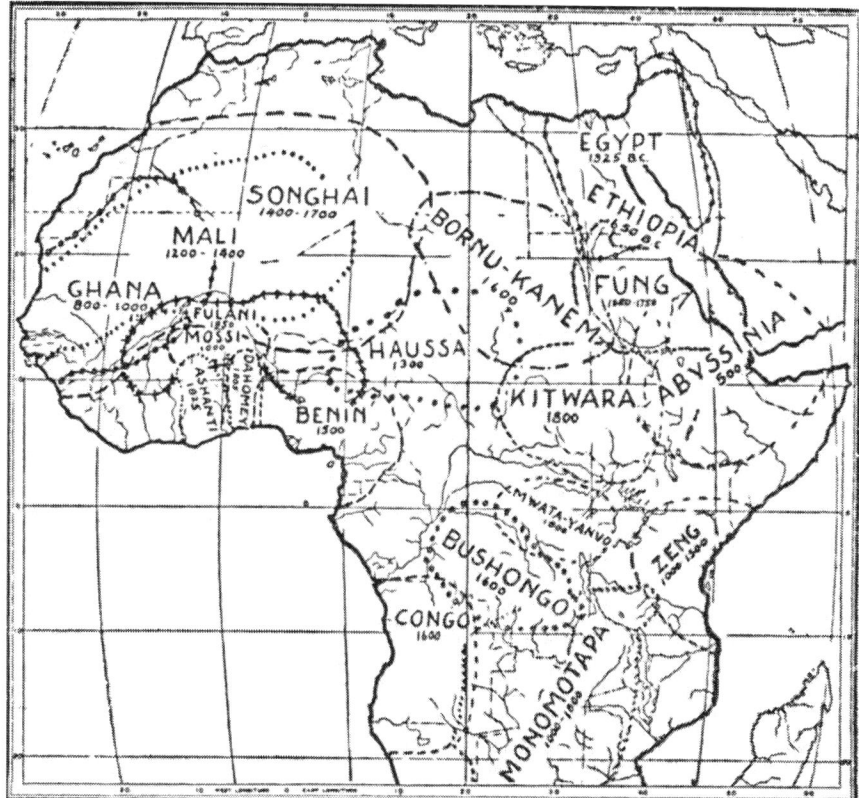

Figure 1. Map of the old African States by Professor W. E. B. Du Bois. Ghana, Mali, Songhai, Ashanti, Hausaland, Benin and Kongo are easily visible. The Nok, Igbo and Ife states are approximately in the same area that Du Bois calls 'Benin'. The Kuba and Shongo cultures are approximately in the area that Du Bois calls 'Bushongo.'

Scripts

The early West Africans had traditions of writing and scholarship. Some of the manuscripts and inscriptions have survived into our times.

The Arabic script was used by the literati of Ancient Ghana, Mali, Songhai, the Ashanti Empire, and the Hausa Confederation. Arabic was the main language of learning occupying a similar place in West Africa to that held by Latin in Europe. However, Professor Ivan Van Sertima, the editor of *Blacks in Science* points out that the Arabic script itself was invented by an Egyptian Negro, Abul Aswan.

Figure 2. The First Sura of the Koran written in Vai.

Many West Africans also used the Arabic letters to write their own languages--this is called Ajami. A number of Ajami manuscripts were written in Songhai, Wolof, Hausa, Fulfulde, Kanuri and Tamasheq.

Other West Africans wrote in scripts with characters of a more pictographic nature. In the early days of the Kingdom of Benin, a 'rude' pictographic script was used. In the regions of Sierra Leone and Liberia, the Vai script was used. This was a wholly alphabetic script and was used in the nineteenth century.

The Adinkra Symbols of the Ashantis have been traced to the script of the ancient people of Libya. Some of these Libyan characters were inherited by the Tuaregs of the Sahara whose script was called Tifinag. Eventually, the characters were inherited by the Akan peoples of Ghana where the symbols were called Adinkra. Incidentally, a script was found among the formerly enslaved Africans in South America called Afaka. Professor Van Sertima believes there was some connection with this script and the Adinkra Symbols. Another scholar, Saki Mafundikwa, traces the origins of Afaka to scripts like the Vai.

According to a seventeenth century writer, hieroglyphics were used in the South West African cultures of Kongo, Ndongo and Matamba.

The Bamoun Kingdom, now in today's Cameroon, has 7,000 surviving manuscripts in their own script.

Finally, some cultures had drum scripts. This is where drummers could copy the patterns of speech and thus convey exact messages in music. The Yorubas and the Ashantis had drum scripts.

Intellectual Culture

In Kumbi-Saleh, capital of the Ancient Ghana Empire, were schools and centres of learning established by at least the eleventh century AD.

In the Mali Empire of the fourteenth century, were two Universities, one at the city of Timbuktu and the other in the city of Djenné.

In the Songhai Empire of the sixteenth century, there were at least three Universities--at Timbuktu, Djenné and Walata. The universities taught law, letters, grammar, geography, mathematical accounting, astronomy and art (which included building and crafts). Professor Ahmed Baba, the last chancellor of the Sankore University Mosque (i.e. Timbuktu) was an excellent example of the calibre of scholar produced in West Africa back in the day. He wrote over 70 books including a biographical dictionary and books on law. He also had a 'small' private library of 1,600 books! The scholars at Timbuktu, for example, noted the appearance of comets, eclipses and earthquakes in the region as mere matters of scientific interest, exciting no great surprise.

In the Hausa territories of northern Nigeria was the University of Katsina. It rose to prominence in about 1600 AD after the fall of Timbuktu. One of their scholars, Ibn Masani, wrote on law, theology, politics, and even on the wonders of Yorubaland. Another scholar, Ibn Muhammad, wrote on mathematical recreations.

The West African scholars and holy men often had vast private libraries. In the time of the Songhai ruler Askiya Daud in the mid sixteenth century, public libraries were established as well. Some of these vast collections have survived into our times. For example, 250,000 old manuscripts have survived in Hausaland. 7,000 manuscripts have survived in Cameroon. 10,000 manuscripts in private collections have survived in the Mauritanian cities of Chinguetti, Walata and Wadan. 11,000 manuscripts in private collections have survived in Niger. Finally, an astonishing 700,000 manuscripts have survived in Timbuktu. Some scholars give even higher figures.

Lost Manuscripts of Chinguetti and Wadan

The Mauritanian city of Chinguetti is an inspiring example of what has survived. The city is home to thousands of centuries old leather-bound tomes passed down from father to son. These pages of fragile parchment are among the oldest surviving examples of writing on paper. Though crinkled and torn, nothing can obscure the flowing lettering in black and golden ink. Some of the books date back to 800 AD having survived the depredations of sand, termites and death-watch beetles. In recent times, the encroachment of Westerners has had an impact. There are scandalous stories of manuscripts being sold off to these people.

Chinguetti is the cultural capital of Mauritania. Founded in the eleventh or twelfth centuries and influenced by the imposing empires of Ancient Ghana, then the Almoravides, and finally Songhai, the city is now under threat. Its young people continue to leave for brighter lights elsewhere and the encroaching desert challenges its physical existence.

In the fourteenth century, the city was home to 40,000 people. Wealth flowed in as camel caravans brought tea, wool and other goods. The nearby salt mine of Idjil was the city's economic mainstay. Scholarship flourished. Chinguetti became a seat of learning renowned for scholars and poets. As typical of much of mediaeval Africa, Arabic became the language of scholarship, just as Latin became the language of the European scholars. Chinguetti became the seventh holiest city in Islam. African pilgrims congregated there before setting off for the Arabian city of Mecca. Twelve mosques thrived, all built in the Western Sudanic architectural style. Today the city's ochre-coloured buildings house around 2,000 people. The trade is now gone, Chinguetti's traditions are dying, and only one of the old mosques is still standing.

Unesco revealed the existence of 3,450 books in Chinguetti and the nearby city of Wadan. Some estimates run as high as 10,000 manuscripts but this figure probably include the manuscripts of Walata, another nearby city, as well. The Chinguetti and Wadan manuscripts are held in 3 libraries and 14 private collections. Mohammed Habott, the Imam of Chinguetti, has a collection of 1,300 books. His ancestors have held and collected books for at least ten generations. The oldest manuscript in his collection dates to 1087 AD and contains one of the world's oldest known drawings of Mecca.

Professor Charles Stewart of Illinois University estimates that one quarter of the books are likely to be about Islamic law. One tenth are likely to be about Sufism, another tenth on Arabic language, another tenth on Koranic studies, another tenth on literature, another tenth on the life and times of the Prophet Mahomet, the founder of Islam, and a tenth on theology. The remaining fifteen percent is likely to cover diverse subjects such as geography, education, encyclopaedias, medicine, astronomy and astrology, mathematics, biographies, ethics, logic and history. Some of the books came from foreign countries in North Africa, also Syria, Arabia and African ruled Spain. Other books are unique to Chinguetti and Wadan.

Ninety percent of the books have seriously deteriorated over the years. Recently, Unesco launched a conservation programme to save the manuscripts. The first stage was to catalogue the books. This is already happening at Nouakchott University in Mauritania's political capital. They have begun the process of putting the manuscripts on to microfilm. The second stage is to treat the damaged books with chemical preservatives. The final stage is to train Mauritanian teams in the skills of manuscript restoration. The originals themselves will stay in Chinguetti and Wadan with their present owners.

Professor Stewart comments that the old libraries 'remain one of the best hidden treasures in Africa.' In truth most Africans, including the scholars, have no idea these manuscripts still exist. Many follow the position of the former Howard University scholar Professor Chancellor Williams in believing that the Arabs destroyed nearly all of this old literature after 1591. Fortunately thousands of texts have survived to this day.

These treasures are of supreme cultural importance to the African world. When catalogued and translated, some of these old books may well contain the African world's Shakespeare, its Da Vinci, its Copernicus, its Martin Luther and its Edward Gibbon. They could form part of an African classical literature to be placed alongside other great African writings from Ancient Egypt, Mediaeval Nubia, Ethiopia, Timbuktu, Hausaland and the Swahili Confederation. This literature could become important in the re-acculturation of all Black people.

The immediate problem is that translations take time and need multidisciplinary teams of scholars to bring the full wealth of the manuscripts before the general public. As Dr Moulaye Hassane, University of Niamey, explains commenting on similar ancient manuscripts from Niger: 'In a 500-page manuscript, you find political, social and religious issues; thus, its exploitation requires the setting up of a multi-disciplinary team of translators, historians, sociologists or anthropologists.'

Such teams cost money. As I write this essay, Unesco and French organisations have already seized the initiative. The lingering question is: Are Black nations willing to finance the recovery and restoration of their ancient and mediaeval culture. So far, only the South Africans have stepped up to the plate.

CHAPTER 1: MATHEMATICS

Introduction

According to Professor Théophile Obenga, the great scholar and historian from Congo, a number of African peoples had sophisticated numerical systems of their own. For example:

o The Yoruba of Nigeria have an indigenous word for 1,000,000 i.e. *egbeeberun.*

o The Ganda of the Great Lakes region have an indigenous word for 20,000,000 i.e. *ebutabalika.*

o The Bakongo of Kasai/Sankuru have an indigenous word for 1,000,000 i.e. *losenene.*

o The Duala of Cameroon have an indigenous pair of words for 3,000,000 i.e. *lodun lolálo.*

o The Fang of Equatorial Guinea have an indigenous phrase for 20,000,000 i.e. *bidudum mewom mebe.*

Professor Obenga regards these examples of evidence that suggests these societies worked with very high numbers, they developed suitable indigenous terminologies for them, and they could thus conceptualise numerically.

Yoruba Numerals

Just imagine having to calculate (200 x 3) - (20 x 4) + 5 before being able to say 'five hundred and twenty five.' According to mathematician, Professor Claudia Zaslavsky, an American specialist on African mathematics, you 'must be a mathematician' to use the Yoruba number system. For this reason, learning Yoruba numerals have a pedagogical value in Nigeria and among some of the African Americans. Educators see the value in teaching this system to pupils since it gets them to use arithmetic in just being able to express the numbers. This system has been in use for hundreds of years and may well date back to the glory days of the Kingdom of Ife.

The Yorubas evolved a complicated numerical system that often involves subtraction and multiplication to express a single number. The Yoruba phrase for three hundred and fifteen is *orin* (which means 20 x 4) *din nirinwo* (from 400) *odin marun* (less 5), which, in mathematical symbols, becomes 400 - (20 x 4) - 5 = 315. The English equivalent 'three hundred and fifteen' is simply (3 x 100) + 15 = 315, making use of multiplication and addition, but no use of subtraction. Many centuries ago, however, when Roman numerals were used across Europe, subtraction was also used. The Roman IV, for example, is 5 - 1, and IX is 10 - 1.

The Yorubas had separate terms for one to ten: i.e. *ookan, eeji, eeta, eerin, aarun, eefa, eeje, eejo, eesan* and *eewaa*. From ten to fourteen, the Yorubas use addition. Their phrase for eleven, for example is *ookan laa,* which is 10 + 1 = 11. The other numbers mean 10 + 2, 10 + 3 and 10 + 4. However for fifteen, they say *eedogun,* which derives from *arun* (five) *din ogun* (from twenty) or 20 - 5 = 15. The other numbers from sixteen to nineteen are 20 - 4, 20 - 3, 20 - 2, and 20 - 1. Between twenty and thirty, there is a similar pattern--addition is used from twenty-one to twenty-four and subtraction is used from twenty-five to twenty-nine. For example, twenty-two becomes 20 + 2 and twenty six becomes 30 - 4.

The Yorubas count in base 20, in contrast to what we use today--base 10. Consequently twenty, and numbers that are multiples of twenty, are important in their system. The word for twenty is *ogun*. The word for forty is *ogoji,* which is derived from *ogun* (twenty) and *eeji* (two). Sixty is *ogota,* derived from *ogun* and *eeta* (three), and eighty (*ogorin*) comes from *ogun* and *eerin* (four). In mathematical symbols 40 = 20 x 2, 60 = 20 x 3 and 80 = 20 x 4. They have special names for important base 20 numbers, such as *igba* (200) and *irinwo* (400), just as the English have special names for important base 10 numbers such as 100 (hundred).

For numbers fifty, seventy and ninety, subtraction is used. The term for fifty is *aadota.* It comes from *ogota,* which, as we have seen, means 20 x 3, and *laa* which is ten, but in this context means minus ten. Fifty is therefore (20 x 3) - 10, seventy is (20 x 4) - 10 and ninety is (20 x 5) - 10. The Yoruba terms for numbers forty-five to forty-nine are complicated, as are sixty-five to sixty-nine and eighty-five to eighty-nine. For example, 46 = (20 x 3) - 10 - 4, 67 = (20 x 4) - 10 - 3 and 88 = (20 x 5) - 10 - 2.

The Yoruba number system had terms for unit fractions 1/2, 1/3, 1/4 and 1/5, etcetera. The Yoruba divination system called the *Odu Ifa* had phrases for 4 raised to the power of 2 (meaning 4 x 4 = 16), 4 raised to the power of 3 (i.e. 4 x 4 x 4 = 64), and 4 raised to the power of 4 (i.e. 4 x 4 x 4 x 4 = 256). The Yorubas also had an indigenous notion of infinity and they had a word for million (*egbeeberun*).

Mathematics in the West African superstates

How is it possible to arrange numbers into a table using each number only once so that each row, each column, and the two diagonals all add up to the same number? This question had intrigued Chinese scholars for thousands of years. However, West African scholars were also interested in this puzzle.

Archaeologists working in the Malian city of Djenné revealed some interesting information:

'In the base of a wall from about A.D. 1400 they found fragments of a type of bowl the Djennenké [i.e. people of Djenné] still place in foundations for protection. One fragment carried magical grids or squares; another was inscribed with a benediction in Arabic; the third had the date 512--or, adjusting from the Islamic calendar, A.D. 1118' (Karen E. Lange, *Djénné: West Africa's Eternal City,* in *National Geographic,* p.110).

Thus, the people of Djenné were familiar with magic squares at least as early as 1400 or even as early as 1118 AD.

What are magic squares? A magic square is a mathematical recreation or game. It is constructed by arranging numbers into a table where each row, each column, and the two diagonals, must add up to the same number

32	14	38	20	44	26	1
48	23	5	29	11	42	17
8	39	21	45	27	2	33
24	6	30	12	36	18	49
40	15	46	28	3	34	9
7	31	13	37	19	43	25
16	47	22	4	35	10	41

Figure 3. A seven order magic square with 175 as the magic constant. All the rows, columns and the two diagonals add up to 175. Notice also that the distance on the squares from '1' to '2' shows the same relationship as the knight's move in chess. Similarly the distance from '2' to '3' also requires a knight's move. This is also true of '3' to '4', '5' to '6', etcetera.

called the magic constant. A Hausa scholar from the University of Katsina, Ibn Muhammad, published a book in 1732 with examples in it. Professor Claudia Zaslavsky made a special study of this manuscript, originally called: *A Treatise on the magical use of the letters of the alphabet.*

Ibn Muhammad worked with three order squares (i.e. 3 x 3 = 9 squares in total), five order squares (i.e. 5 x 5 = 25 squares in total) right up to eleven order squares (i.e. 11 x 11 = 121 squares in total).

He also demonstrated how a given magic square can be reflected about the vertical axis, the horizontal axis, and about the two diagonals. Moreover, he showed how a given square can be rotated through 90 degrees, 180 degrees and 270 degrees.

Professor Claudia Zaslavsky, mentioned earlier, shows that a magic square of odd number n (3, 5, 7, etc.), consists of a square array of numbers from 1 to n^2, then the magic constant will be equal to $n(n^2 + 1) \div 2$. For example, if we try to construct a seven order magic square (7 x 7 = 49), then n = 7. This means that the numbers used will be 1 to 7^2 (= 49) and the magic constant will be $7(7^2 + 1) \div 2 = 175$.

Commenting on this, Professor Finch, an authority on African science history, noted that this shows 'the "algebraic" quality of magic squares and why a sound knowledge of number theory is important in their creation.' This raises the question: Did West Africans only get as far as algebra?

A *New Scientist* article had plenty to say on the practise of mathematics at Timbuktu which answers this question:

'[T]he Muslim scholars of Timbuktu would … have had particular reasons to be interested in astronomy. First is the requirement for Muslims to pray, and to orient their mosques in the direction of Mecca. To achieve this, they needed to develop algorithms and instruments to determine the exact position of both Mecca and Timbuktu. There was also the need to determine exact times for prayers at sunrise, noon, afternoon, sunset and evening. The scholars found ancient Greek methods of doing this very cumbersome, the researchers say, but Muslim astronomers devised easier solutions by inventing the cosine, tangent, cotangent, secant and cosecant functions of trigonometry.'

Moreover, mathematics was one of the liberal arts taught at the Songhai universities. The scholars, Hunwick and Boye, state that Timbuktu scholars purchased and copied manuscripts on geometry and calculus. Finally, Professor Henry Louis Gates, the famous African American academic, drew attention to a surviving manuscript in a Timbuktu library on mathematical accounting.

Geometry

It may seem the height of disrespect to compare the old and exquisite Benin Bronzes or the fabulous Congolese Textiles to wallpaper, but there is a connection. Wallpaper, despite its apparent blandness, is actually a treasure trove of applied mathematical techniques. Typical wallpaper designs are based on a single idea or motif that is repeated across the paper using two geometric operations, translation and reflection.

Translation is where a motif is repeated by moving it in a straight line from its original position to position one, two, three, four, etcetera. Reflection is where a motif is repeated as if it were a mirror image of the original. Reflection can take place along a vertical axis, making the left hand side of the original motif, the right hand side of the reflected motif. It can also take place along a horizontal axis, making the bottom of the original motif the top of the reflected motif.

There are 24 different combinations of translation and/or reflection (including rotating the motif by 60 degrees, 90 degrees, 120 degrees, 180 degrees or 360 degrees) that can be used to cover a wall. The proof that there were only 24 such techniques allegedly came from a scholar called Federov in 1891. An analysis of Islamic art, however, proved that the Islamic world had long made use of all 24 techniques. This raised the question of whether this knowledge existed in West and Central African arts and crafts.

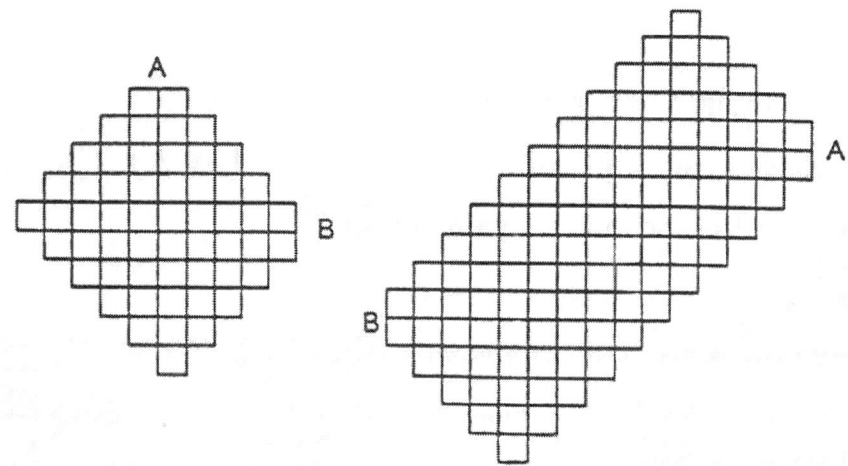

Figure 4. In order to draw these networks, one must start at the entry points A or B.

Dr D. W. Crowe and Professor Zaslavsky made independent studies of the Benin Bronzes of the Nigeria region and the Bakuba Textiles from the Congo region. The Benin masterpieces were mostly from the sixteenth century and the Congolese crafts were mostly from the eighteenth century. Dr Crowe concluded that 17 of the 24 possible mathematical techniques appeared in the Benin Bronzes, and 'at least' 19 of the 24 techniques appeared in the Bakuba Textiles.

Other uses of geometry are demonstrated by a game traditionally played by Shongo children in the Congo region. According to mathematician Professor Beatrice Lumpkin, the game involved drawing complex networks with a continuous line or path, without taking one's pen or pencil off the page and without tracing the same line twice. A European mathematician, Leonhard Euler developed solutions to this problem in 1735. He also established a new branch of topology called network analysis. However, according to Professor Lumpkin, it is likely that the Shongo games are much older than the time of Euler.

Figure 5. The Rao Pectoral, twelfth or thirteenth century AD. 22 carat gold, 18 cm in diameter.

Finally, West Africans (and Africans elsewhere) made practical use of fractal geometry. Fractals are characterised by repeated geometric patterns over ever diminishing scales. The Rao Pectoral was a magnificent golden artefact buried with a vassal prince of Ancient Ghana from the twelfth or thirteenth centuries AD. This pectoral uses the circle over and over at different scales, offering a pleasing aesthetic. Professor Ron Eglash, an expert on fractals, shows that Africans used fractal geometry in architectural ornamentation, architectural plans, and even in hair braiding!

I have written more information on these topic areas in a book co authored by John Matthews entitled *African Mathematics: History, Textbook and Classroom Lessons* (UK, Reklaw Education, 2014, pp.58-86).

CHAPTER 2: ASTRONOMY AND PHYSICS

Astronomy among the Dogon

The Dogon are a non Islamic people in modern Mali. Their knowledge has created quite a stir since the early nineteenth century. They traditionally taught their initiates about the Rings of Saturn, four of the (nine) Moons of Jupiter, the spiral structure of the Milky Way Galaxy, and the desolate surface of the Moon.

Dogon knowledge was revealed to the world through the writings of a French initiate into the Dogon system, Marcel Griaule, who wrote up the information in a book called *The Pale Fox.*

How far back do Dogon calculations go? The Dogon have a tradition of choosing a new priest every 60 years at the SIGUI festival. This is where the orbits of Jupiter and Saturn synchronize. Based on the number of changes of priests and other cultural data, most writers date the Dogon

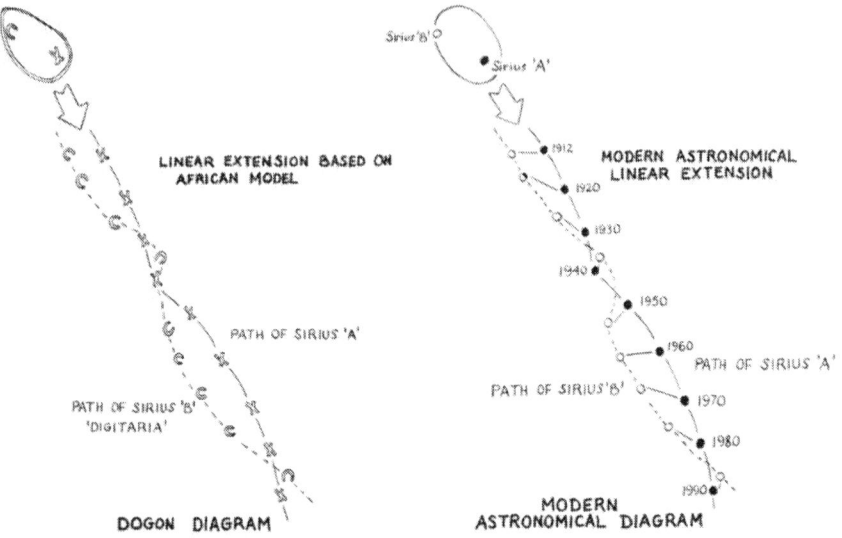

Figure 6. Sketch drawn in the sand by Dogon elders to initiates concerning Sirius A and B compared to the ideas of modern astronomers.

knowledge to the early 1200s AD. Thus the Dogon were a part of the histories of the Mediaeval Mali and Songhai Empires. However, linguists point out that the Dogon language, and thus the Dogon culture is very ancient indeed.

The Dogon evolved a 354 day lunar calendar, a 365 day solar calendar, a Sirius calendar which implies (but does not prove) a 365.25 day calendar, and a Venusian agricultural calendar based on observing the six positions or phases of the planet Venus.

The Dogon have sophisticated ideas based on a star called Sirius 'B.' Sirius B is a star that orbits Sirius. To the unaided eye, it is invisible. The Dogon elders maintain that it is the smallest and densest type of star in our galaxy, an idea confirmed by modern astronomy. The Dogon say that Sirius B orbits Sirius every 50 years, also confirmed by modern astronomy.

Controversially, the Dogon say that Sirius B rotates on its own axis each year and they celebrate this at the BADO celebration. They also say that another companion star, Sirius C, is four times larger than Sirius B. Modern astronomers cannot confirm or deny these propositions and so the jury is still out. Whichever be the case, Professor Finch says: 'it is the Dogon who deserve credit for having discovered Sirius B and the white dwarf as a category of star.'

The Dogon today are a relatively poor and isolated population. This raised the question of: How did the Dogon know any of this advanced scientific knowledge?

Mr Hunter Havelin Adams III, an African American authority on African and African American science history, believes that the Dogon have inherited part of the knowledge acquired from the astronomers and mathematicians at the Mediaeval West African University of Timbuktu. I believe that it could just have easily been the other way round. It could be that the Timbuktu scholars learned their ideas from the Dogon.

Astronomy at Timbuktu

Michael Palin, in his TV series *Sahara,* said the imam of Timbuktu: 'has a collection of scientific texts that clearly show the planets circling the sun. They date back hundreds of years ... Its convincing evidence that the scholars of Timbuktu knew a lot more than their counterparts in Europe. In the fifteenth century in Timbuktu the mathematicians knew about the rotation of the planets, knew about the details of the eclipse, they knew things which we had to wait for 150 almost 200 years to know in Europe when Galileo and Copernicus came up with these same calculations and were given a very hard time for it.'

However, not all scholars are agreed with all of this. A *New Scientist* article gave the following information on Timbuktu Astronomy:

'While they may have got it wrong about the motion of the planets, the manuscript reveals that the scholars had precise methods for defining the Islamic calendar, including algorithms on how to determine leap years. The algorithms were as accurate as anything mathematicians have today, as Medupe found when he tested them against the modern, computer-based approach. "These people were very knowledgeable about the subject they wrote about," he says. Other manuscripts dating back 600 years include beautifully drawn diagrams of the orbits of planets, which demonstrate the use of complex mathematical calculations. There are also recordings of astronomical events, including a meteor shower in August 1583. Another manuscript discusses the use of an astronomical instrument to determine the direction of Mecca.'

What is at issue here between Palin and the writer at *New Scientist* is that SOME Timbuktu manuscripts have the EARTH as the centre of the Solar System and not the sun. However, both men are agreed that Timbuktu mathematicians had calculated the orbits of the planets well over a century before Galileo and Copernicus.

Professor Rodney Thebe Medupe, a South African astrophysicist, is the leading authority on Timbuktu Astronomy. He wrote the 2009 film documentary *The Ancient Astronomers of Timbuktu*. He illustrated a number of astronomical themes in the documentary using specific Timbuktu manuscripts, such as:

'The direction to Mecca--the qibla--for the five daily prayers, using spherical trigonometry and a simpler method using the gnomon.

Calendars--the lunar and solar calendar systems and the difference between various calendars around the world.

A method to calculate leap years.

Sine quadrant--using information from a manuscript the researchers use a quadrant to tell the time by measuring the angle of the Sun.

Information from a manuscript to show how to use the 28 lunar mansions to tell the time at night.

A copy of a manuscript with tables originally written by a renowned medieval Egyptian astronomer with calculations and information on the positions of the planets, moon and stars.'

Dogon Physics

The Dogon have a concept called *po*. It is the smallest cultivated seed (*digitaria exilis*) and has several symbolic meanings for the Dogon. *The Pale Fox,* the work written by the French initiate into the Dogon system has the following about the *po*:

'This internal movement of the smallest of all the elements God created is reflected in space by the spiralling motion of the stars' (*The Pale Fox,* p.445).

Clearly, the Dogon are using the concept of *po* as an atom with its internal movements being likened to that of a micro solar system.

Another Dogon idea concerns Dada the spider. In their symbolic thought, he wove the words of Ogo, the Master of Chaos, in the acacia tree as the universe was being formed. *The Pale Fox* says:

'Placed at the center of the acacia, the spider wove its threads in a conical spiral for the placement of the warp, and by moving vertically for the coming and going of the passing woof ... Through the fabric, it sifted the germs that had been hurled into the universe by spinning' (Ibid., p.236).

This extract suggests that the Dogon had radical ideas about how we should conceptualise matter. Increasingly since 1984, avant-garde physicists have developed new theories to explain matter that contrast with the prevailing particle theories. Called 'string' theories, the physicists who advocate these models say that matter is better conceptualised as a composition of strands that have no dimensions except length instead of as isolated particles. Some of these physicists even use terms that liken the interconnections between matter to those of a spider's web. Some speak of a 'cosmic cobweb'. Others speak of a 'cosmic web.'

A third example of Dogon thought is illustrated by the following thee excerpts:

'[T]he bursting of the *po* and the whirling of the spiral in the other direction made [Amma's seat] pivot ... although Amma created the world, he made the *po* responsible for putting it into motion: by whirling and then acting as a spring, the *po* took along and then distributed all things in the universe' (Ibid., p.423).

'The star's former position in space is where now the sun is ... Like the other stars, it moved away ... but it is a center in motion' (Ibid., p.505).

Also: '[T]he universe in Amma's womb was still outside of time and space, which were intermingled' (Ibid., p.201).

These extracts suggest that the Dogon had a notion of big bang derived from a singularity. Singularity is the idea that the universe began as a single tiny speck where the laws of time and space do not yet exist. It is the explosion of this kernel, i.e. big bang, that led to the creation of the universe where time and space exists.

The Dogon had other highly abstract ideas that would not seem dated, even today:

'The number 14, attributed to the spiral stellar worlds produced by Amma, implies the concept of potential reproduction and multiplication: seven is the sum of three, the masculine number, and four, the feminine number ... The superposition of worlds and the concept of the infinite multiplication of stellar universes are indicated by the fact that the number 28 is attributed to Amma as well; it is called "Amma's number" ... The spiral worlds of stars were populated universes' (Ibid., pp.193-4).

This suggests that the Dogon had notions of 28 multiple and even parallel universes (incidentally with intelligent life forms).

CHAPTER 3: HOW DEEP DID DOGON KNOWLEDGE GO?

Introduction

Marcel Griaule and Germain Dieterlen, two pioneering anthropologists, were highly impressed by the sophisticated belief systems of the Dogon initiates. In a 1954 essay, they wrote the following: '[W]ithin and beyond this totality of beliefs appears a logical scheme of symbols expressing a system of thought which cannot be described simply as myth. For this conceptual structure, when studied, reveals an internal coherence, a secret wisdom, and an apprehension of ultimate realities equal to that which we Europeans conceive ourselves to have attained' (Marcel Griaule & Germaine Dieterlen, *The Dogon,* in *African Worlds,* p.83).

In my opinion, this is a BIG STATEMENT that should not be taken lightly. I recommend that you, the reader, re-read this statement by Griaule and Dieterlen before contemplating the rest of this chapter.

Carl Sagan, a great astrophysicist and populariser of science, was much less positive, however. While he concedes that the Dogon had a 'cluster of hard scientific knowledge' ... 'preserved by oral tradition over the millennia, and only in West Africa' (Quoted in Hunter Havelin Adams III, *African Observers of the Universe: The Sirius Question,* in *Blacks in Science,* p.37), he unsuccessfully argues that the Dogon must have been taught this information by a scientifically literate European! Kenneth Brecher, a scientist at the Massachusetts Institute of Technology, was equally blunt. He stated that the Dogon 'have no business knowing any of this' (Quoted in ibid., p.32). Other writers, perhaps inspired by science fiction writers like Erich Von Daniken, claimed that the Dogon knowledge base proves that extra terrestrials existed and it was *they* who taught the Dogon this knowledge!

Laird Scranton, a European American researcher, made a special study of the two most important texts on Dogon knowledge *Conversations with Ogotemmeli* and *The Pale Fox.* Some of his findings resemble and echo those of Professor Charles Finch. However, some of his conclusions resemble those of the writers mentioned above--i.e. a general disbelief that the Dogon could have produced these ideas by themselves without extra terrestrial help.

Which ever be the case, Scranton began by comparing Dogon ideas of the natural water cycle with scientific ones contained in the scholarly literature. In *Conversations with Ogotemmeli,* we read: 'The life-force of the earth is water. God moulded the earth with water. Blood too he made out of water. Even in a stone there is this force, for there is moisture in everything ... When the sky is overcast, the sun's rays may be seen materializing on the misty horizon. These rays ... are water, too, because they uphold the earth's moisture as it rises' (p.19). Scranton consulted an entry in an *Encyclopaedia Britannica* on water and found that the article reaffirmed that living matter is made up principally of water, as are the life giving fluids of animals and plants. Water settles in rocks beneath the earth and is present in rocks themselves. Moreover, water vapour rises due to the action of the sun and fell back to earth as rain. Scranton concluded that these comparisons showed the Dogon ideas contained good scientific information that could be pursued further.

Drawing a bigger conclusion, Scranton believes that the Dogon creation stories contained a mythological storyline that, on the surface, narrated the building blocks of civilisation. These building blocks were acquiring a language, wearing clothing, the skills of weaving, pottery, agriculture and metallurgy, living in a family structure, creating a community structure, and building houses and storage facilities. However, underneath this surface storyline, according to Scranton, were two deep scientific narratives. One of these outlined Dogon ideas on the origin and structure of matter, the other outlined Dogon ideas on sexual reproduction.

Deep Storyline One: The Structure of Matter

The Dogon creation story begins with Amma's egg that refers to the unformed universe. When this opens, the first thing to come out of it is the *po*. Scranton believes the unformed universe is a black hole, and the *po* represents an atom. As we have seen, Professor Finch presents evidence that supports this view. While Finch stops here, Scranton believes Dogon ideas delve deeper into smaller and smaller building blocks. For instance, the Dogon have a story connected to *sene* seeds. Scranton believes these ideas approximately correspond to the electrons, protons and neutrons of modern chemistry. In support of his idea, he notices the similarity between Dogon drawings of the *sene,* and the orbits of electrons around the nucleus of an atom. The Dogon also speak of the combinations of *sene* seeds at the center of the *po* which seem similar to the combinations of protons and neutrons to form the nucleus of atoms.

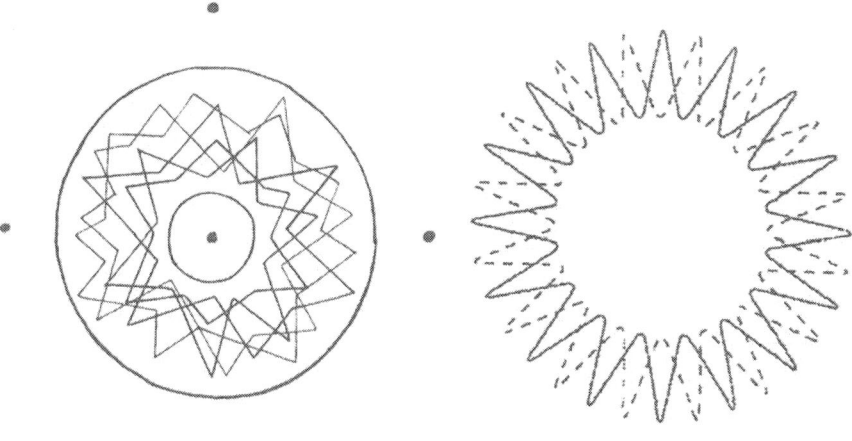

Figure 7. Is there any connection between the Dogon drawing on the left with the vibratory pattern of a string on the right?

The Dogon creation story speaks of the germination of the *sene* seed. They represent these using 4 different drawn symbols. Scranton believes the germination of the *sene* seed represents the components of electrons, protons and neutrons. He thinks the 4 drawn symbols resemble the 4 classes of quantum particles that combine to form the smaller elements within an atom. Professor Stephen Hawkins, the great populariser of abstract scientific ideas, explained that quantum particles can be divided into 4 classes based on a quality called 'spin'. 'Spin,' in this context, refers to the appearance of a particle if you turned it around. One group of particles look the same from all sides. A second group look the same if you turn it half way around. A third group look the same if you turn it all the way around. A fourth group look the same if you turn it all the way around twice. Scranton believes that the 4 *sene* germination drawings are a Dogon attempt to capture these or equivalent ideas.

The Dogon creation story speaks of 266 signs. Scranton believes these signs represent the 200 plus elementary types of particles of matter. The difference is that scientists are unsure of the figure but the Dogon think there are 266.

Finally, the Dogon creation story speaks of Dada the spider who weaves cosmic patterns. They use drawings to represents this concept. Scranton believes that beneath the idea of the 200 plus elementary types of particles of matter are the vibrations of cosmic strings. Professor Charles Finch has long published his ideas on the connection between Dada the spider and string theory. Scranton compares one of the Dogon drawings with diagrams teachers use today to represent quantum strings and notes a startling similarity with one such diagram.

Deep Storyline Two: Sexual Reproduction

The Dogon stories link Amma's egg with a human womb. Griaule and Dieterlen wrote: 'Amma's egg is represented in the form of an oblong picture, with signs, called "womb of all world signs," the centre of which is the umbilicus … The oval contained the 266 "signs of Amma"' (Quoted in Laird Scranton, *The Science of the Dogon,* pp.110-111). The oblong picture to which they refer is a drawing that the Dogon used to explain this concept. Scranton believes this all represents sexual reproduction. He compares the spiral structure in the drawing to the spiral helix of DNA. This is an opinion shared by Professor Charles Finch. Scranton also believes the 266 seeds must represent genes and the chromosomes in which they were contained.

It is well known that the Dogon consider the number 3 to be a male number and the number 4 to be a female number. Scranton believes that the three represents the apparent number of branches in a Y chromosome, and the four represents the apparent number of branches in an X chromosome.

CHAPTER 4: METALLURGY

Metallurgy in the Coastal States

Metallurgy was always a highly skilled and specialised craft. The associated skills include the difficult and dangerous skill of mining and the sophisticated skill of prospecting. Some of the earliest metallurgical evidence in West Africa includes a group of iron and copper tools excavated in Senegal dated at 2800 BC also iron smelting in Nok (ancient Nigeria) by 2000 BC. At the Nok sites, blast furnaces and tuyères were found. Tuyères are pipes used to conduct air and thus raise temperatures in the metal smelting process.

Figure 8. Superb vessel in the shape of a sea shell from Igbo-Ukwu, ninth or tenth century AD. Leaded bronze. Length 20.6 cm.

Metallurgy reached a high point in ninth century AD Eastern Nigeria at a civilisation archaeologists call Igbo-Ukwu. Here, astounding evidence of leaded bronze art and craft were recovered. Leaded bronze is an alloy of copper, tin, lead and silver worked together. The splendid craft pieces were made using the six-stage lost wax technique.

The lost wax technique involves (i) making a rough clay model of the artefact to be made, (ii) placing a layer of bees wax over the model with all the fine and intricate details, perhaps keeping the wax 3 mm thick, (iii) placing a second layer of clay over the bees wax, (iv) placing everything into a kiln and fire it knowing that the melting point of wax is lower than the melting point of clay--the molten wax runs out leavening a 3 mm gap, (v) pouring molten metal(s) into the mould replacing the 'lost' molten wax, and (vi) waiting for the molten metal to cool and harden into shape followed by removing the layers of clay. Incidentally, this is the same technique used today to make car parts.

The court art of the Yoruba Kingdom of Ife (eleventh to fifteenth century AD) and the Empire of Benin (sixteenth and seventeenth century) is amongst the very best in the world. Like at Igbo-Ukwu, these kingdoms used the lost wax technique to make the Ife and Benin Bronzes. Art historians prefer the term 'bronzes', but strictly speaking many of the Ife and Benin masterpieces were actually of brass, zinc brass or copper. Copper is a particularly difficult metal to flow through a mould, thus these pieces are not only artistic masterpieces but also technological masterworks.

One of these pieces from the fourteenth century shows a soldier wearing chainmail. Songhai records mention helmets, gauntlets and body armour. *On the Obligations of Princes,* a late fifteenth century Hausa text, mentions body armour. Chainmail was also used by soldiers in Benin, the Central Saharan Empire of Kanem-Borno and also Sudan on the Upper Nile.

The Yoruba Kingdom of Old Oyo produced iron and steel using very complex technologies that were as advanced as the steel produced on the East African coast of the early mediaeval period. Many writers are now conceding that these East African techniques were the most sophisticated in the world before the end of the nineteenth century. Clearly the techniques used in Old Oyo were equally sophisticated.

Iron was worked extensively in the Kongo and the Ndongo and Matamba (i.e. in modern Angola) regions in the fifteenth century onwards. The craft of the blacksmith accorded high status to its members. However, linguists working with the Kongolese and other Bantu languages have traced many

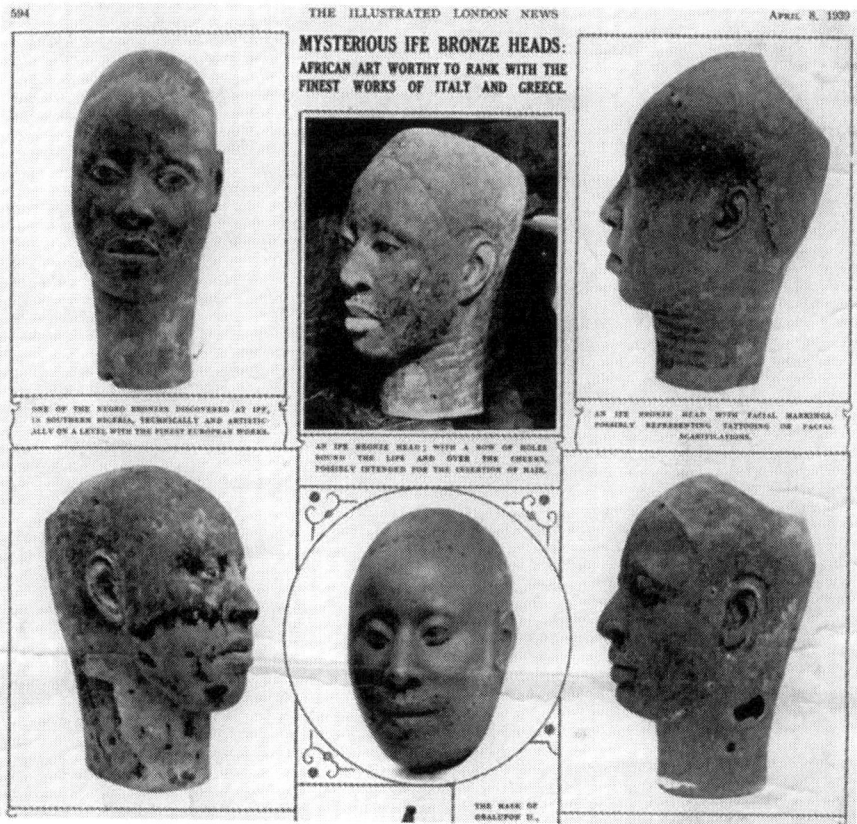

Figure 9. Page from *The Illustrated London News* (8 April 1939) reporting on 'Mysterious Ife Bronze Heads: African art worthy to rank with the finest works of Italy and Greece.' These metal masterpieces date from the eleventh to the fifteenth centuries AD.

words to do with metallurgy in their languages back to perhaps 3000 BC. If the words existed back then, then the metallurgical practices must also have existed as well! Whichever be the case, Kongolese metallurgists were well aware of the problems posed by working with lead and had preventative and curative means of combating lead poisoning.

Gold was panned, mined and intricately worked in the Akan and later the Ashanti region of today's Ghana. Giving some idea of the scale of the gold working, one scholar reported that 15 shiploads of local gold were seized by the Portuguese in 1502. The Akan and Ashanti pieces were exquisite works of art and ornamentation. They made bracelets, necklaces, gold decorated weaponry and gold decorated sandals.

Metallurgy in the West African Superstates

Gold mining in the Ancient Ghana region (now today's Mauritania and Mali) dates back to the fourth century AD. Gold (and sometimes silver) was used to make swords, shields, bracelets, bells and was turned into thread to embroider cloth. By the twelfth century, gold was minted into coins. The Moors introduced this coinage into Europe that century, which started a trend for gold coins. Mints were established in Northern Spain in the thirteenth century, then Northern Europe in the fourteenth century. One particularly fine piece of Ghanaian gold work is the famous Rao Pectoral found in a twelfth or thirteenth century burial (see page 18).

In Mali, the successor empire, court musicians had instruments covered in gold and silver. The Hall of Audience in Niani, a fourteenth century architectural wonder, had windows with gold and silver frames. In Songhai, the successor empire, the royalty used utensils all covered in gold. The total amount of gold mined to the year 1500 was very conservatively estimated at $35 billion at 1998 gold prices reflecting the combined output of Ancient Ghana, Mali and Songhai. The empires of Ghana, Mali and Songhai had huge golden nuggets and other golden artefacts. Leo Africanus, a sixteenth century visitor, reports that one such golden piece weighed 1300 Ibs and was in the possession of the Emperor of Songhai.

As late as 1790, Senegalese gold and silversmiths were still supreme. They produced finer gold and silver work than anyone in Europe at the time. A witness at a British Government Select Committee on the Slave Trade testified to this effect on 29 April 1790.

CHAPTER 5: MEDICINE AND SURGERY

Songhai

In 1420 a Songhai doctor, Aben Ali, successfully treated the French crown prince, later King Charles VII when everybody else failed. Secondly, in 1492 the great Songhai emperor Sunni Ali Ber was mummified. These two examples tell us something of the high standards of medical and surgical knowledge in West Africa in the fifteenth century.

Mahmud Kati, a Songhai historian, mentions the use of locally manufactured soap. A surviving sixteenth century Timbuktu manuscript has a formula for making toothpaste and adds that regular brushing of your teeth removes bad breath. Other surviving manuscripts deal with chemistry, traditional medicines and pharmacopoeia.

Moreover, Professor Diop shows how the West Africans organised medical practice at that time: 'Empirical medicine was quite developed in Africa … a family practised a single branch of medicine on an hereditary basis. One was specialised in the eyes, the stomach, and so on.'

West Africa

Dr Charles Finch, associate professor of medicine at Morehouse, demonstrated that West African countries traditionally used a large range of plants, minerals and animal material for medical purposes. Some groups, such as the Mano of Liberia, even practiced quarantining to contain diseases. West Africans traditionally used local anaesthetics and had treatments for asthma, bronchitis, diabetes, malaria and muscular-skeletal pain. They used plants that had anti-sickle cell properties and other plants that had insect repellent properties.

Azadirachta indica, or the Neem tree, grows widely across Africa. Healers traditionally used its bark and leaves to treat malaria and to reduce muscular-skeletal pain. Tinctures derived from the Neem tree have greater anti-inflammatory properties than aspirin. *Bridelia ferruginea* is an effective treatment for diabetes. One study produced examples where some patients' blood sugar levels returned to normal after taking the treatment for twelve weeks. *Zanthoxulum zanthoxlides,* or the chewing stick, effectively cleans teeth and combats tooth decay. It also has anti sickle-cell properties. *Ocimum gratissimum* treats diarrhoea. It also has insect repellent properties. For this reason, many people grew this plant near their homes. *Pergularia daema* has multiple uses. It functioned as a post-circumcision anaesthetic. It was also a topical treatment for abscesses and wounds. Finally, *Euphorbita hirta* treats asthma and bronchitis.

One specific example concerns the Yoruba of Ijebu and the Ijo. They practiced massage, bone surgery and herbalism to a highly developed degree. They washed then bandaged dead bodies in layers and layers of bandages and cloth with the two hands of the dead individual brought together.

Another specific example was in the Kingdom of Senegal. A European testified at a British Government Select Committee in 1790 that Senegalese physicians had a of 2,000 or nearly 3,000 plants. This, incidentally, is a pharmacopoeia two and a half times as extensive as that of the Ancient Egyptians.

It may surprise most readers but it remains a fact that the majority of enslaved Africans were inoculated against smallpox BEFORE they were deported from Africa. The Mano of Liberia were among a number of West African peoples that invented a smallpox vaccine before the Europeans. Susan McIntosh and Roderick McIntosh, both experts on Ancient Mali, state that West African blacksmiths, such as the Bambara, also developed a smallpox vaccine before the Europeans. One enslaved African in Boston, Onesimus, taught the treatment to his enslaver in the 1720s.

The University of Djenné taught surgery in mediaeval times. One area of specialism was eye cataract surgery.

CHAPTER 6: BOAT BUILDING AND NAVIGATION

Malians in Panama

Boat building took place in the Niger, Senegal and Kongo regions. The main boats were barges or gondoliers. Some could carry 80 people. The larger crafts were 100 feet long, 14 feet across and drew seven feet of water. They had decks and a central cabin. Professor Cheikh Anta Diop and Michael Bradley speculate that many of the earlier crafts possessed sails.

A Syrian scholar, Shihab al-Din Ibn Fadl Al-Umari, published *Masalik ab Absar fi Mamalik al Amsar,* in Cairo 1342. Chapter X of this book mentions two royal Malian voyages across the Atlantic involving hundreds of vessels. Apparently 400 ships laden with water and gold sailed west from the Senegambian coast. In a second voyage, 2,000 ships sailed west with water and supplies led by the 'predecessor of Sultan Musa.' Malian oral traditions identify the king as Mansa Abubakari II. He may well have commanded these voyages in perhaps 1310 or 1311 AD.

Figure 10. Detail of a Kongolese scene drawn in the seventeenth century showing Kongolese watercraft of various types.

Were such large fleets common in West Africa at that time? Professor Cheikh Anta Diop in *Precolonial Black Africa* divides West African vessels into *almadias* that could carry from 3 to 50 people, and *kantas* that could carry up to 80 people. Mahmud Kati, author of the sixteenth century chronicle *Tarikh al-Fettash,* recorded that Mansa Musa I used a 'large number' of almadias to transport people and luggage from Timbuktu to Niani on the Niger in connection with his 1324 pilgrimage to Mecca. The same author recorded that Askiya Ishaq II used 3,000 *almadias* to evacuate Gao during the Arab/European invasion in 1591.

Maps indicate that the Malians (also called Mandingas) got to Panama (in Central America) and renamed places after themselves. For example 'Mali' is a place in Africa. Compare with 'Sierre de Mali' a name once given to a mountain range in Darien, Panama. Another example is 'Mandinga' which is a language and cultural identifier in Africa. Compare with 'Mandinga Port' and 'Mandinga Bay', former place names in Panama. Scholars noticed these place names appearing on maps such as the map by Lopéz, *Atlas de la América,* published in Paris, 1758. These place names were used until the mid nineteenth century.

Inscriptions have been found that indicate that the Malians got to the Danish Virgin Islands. One often quoted inscription written in Tifinag read as follows: 'Plunge in to clear away impurities. This is water for ablutions.' The Tuaregs of the Sahara used this script.

The Smithsonian Institute made an important discovery in 1974 and 1975. They found two African skeletons at Hull Bay, Danish Virgin Islands, dating to around 1250 AD. While this date is 61 years away from the 1311 date for Abubakari II, many scholars connect the two since all dating systems have a plus or minus error range.

Finally, the view that West Africans had visited the Americas before Columbus was conceded by Columbus himself. One piece of evidence that was particularly startling was the fact that Columbus collected samples of gold alloyed javelins from the Native Americans which, when he had them checked out in Spain, on his return, were found to have been made of an alloy manufactured only in West Africa.

Yorubas and Ancient America

Professor Ekpo Eyo, a leading authority on Nigerian antiquities, narrated a curious oral tradition concerning Oni Oluwo, a distinguished Yoruba ruler. Apparently she was walking around the capital when her regalia got splashed with mud. Oluwo was so upset by this that she ordered the construction of pavements for all the public and religious places in the city (figure 12).

Professor Leo Frobenius was a pioneering German Africanist. He was impressed by African culture, and firmly believed that Africans contributed much to the onward march of civilisation. In 1913 when Professor Frobenius aired his ideas many thought that he was crazy. For instance he believed that there was a connection between the Yoruba civilisation and the Mayans of Ancient America. In his own words:

'I cannot finish without devoting a word or two to a certain symptomatic conformity of the Western Atlantic civilisation with its higher manifestations in America. Its cognate features are so striking that they cannot be overlooked, and as the region of Atlantic African culture is Yoruba ... it seems to be a present question, whether it might not be possible to bring the marvellous Maya monuments ... into some prehistoric connection with those of Yoruba.'

Strangely enough, archaeology has supported some of Frobenius' ideas. For example, Dr David Kelley wrote:

'The kind of evidence field archaeologists like is the pavement of Île Ife, a former Yoruba capital ... This is made from broken potsherds that were decorated by rolling corncobs over their surface before firing. Paul Mangelsdorf, who had seen some of the sherds assured me (about 1954) that they were indeed Zea mays [i.e. an American plant]. Another interpretation of Yoruba tradition is that the capital was moved from Île Ife to Old Oyo about A.D. 1100 or earlier ... If so, this site provides the hard evidence that archaeologists want for American plants in Africa in pre-Columbian times' (David Kelley quoted in Ivan Van Sertima, *Early America Revisited,* p.7).

What conclusions should we draw? This evidence suggests that either the Yorubas sailed to the Mayan territories in 1100 AD or even earlier to collect the corncobs. Another possibility is that Mayans sailed to Yorubaland and delivered the corncobs. Whichever way it happened, connections between the Mayans and the Yorubas were indeed forged around 1100 AD or earlier. This is hundreds of years before Columbus sailed in 1492.

CHAPTER 7: ARCHITECTURE

Architecture in the West African Superstates

Ancient Ghana (in the period 700-1200 AD) dominated the same area as modern Mali and Mauritania. The empire, at its height, even ruled the Senegal, Gambia and Guinea regions. Ghana's main cities were Nema, Walata, Audoghast and Kumbi-Saleh (the capital). Archaeological excavations of Kumbi-Saleh uncovered large houses (up to nine rooms) almost habitable today for want of renovation, several stories high with underground rooms, staircases and connecting halls. The masonry was excellent, with walls 30 cm thick. The Emperors of the twelfth century lived in a castle thoroughly fortified, with sculptures, paintings and glass windows. Kumbi-Saleh had a population several times greater than 30,000 people (cf. London's fourteenth century total of 20,000). Divided into two townships by religion, its suburbs had houses surrounded by gardens. Moreover, the non-Muslim part of the city had domed buildings indicating that domes were part of traditional non-Muslim architecture.

Mali, the successor empire, continued the architectural tradition but advanced it in the area of planning. It was common to find wide, straight thoroughfares lined on both sides by trees. In the fourteenth century, the great cities of Timbuktu, Djenné and Niani, its capital, dominated national life. The Hall of Audience, a Niani monument built by Mansa Musa I, was

Figure 11. There are some bizarre and futuristic architectural pieces from this part of the world. This village from Cameroon was photographed in 1912. No-one seems to know how old this architectural tradition was but it certainly predates the coming of the Europeans.

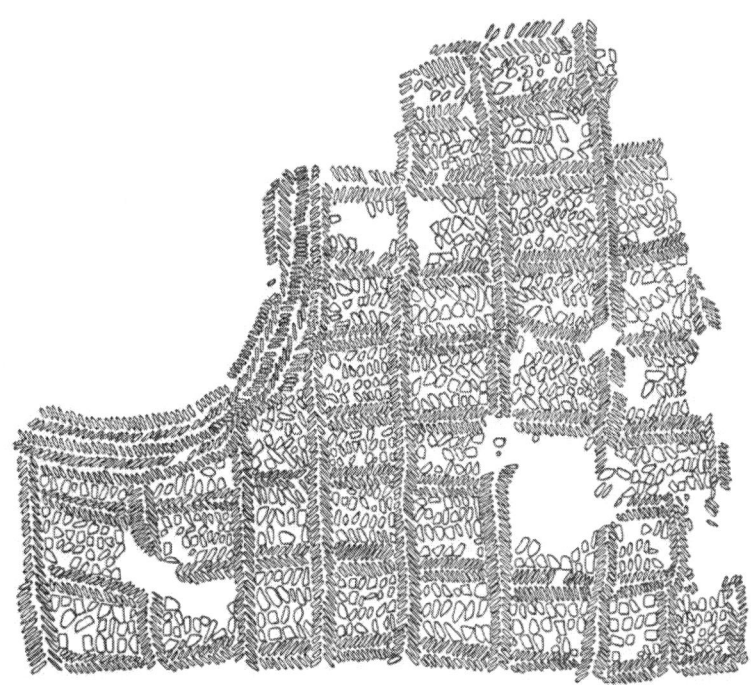

Figure 12. Sketch of an excavated Ile-Ife pavement from *c.*1000 AD by Susan Denyer showing chevron patterns forming squares with quartz pebbles set inside each square. American corncobs were used to make the chevron patterns.

a building made of cut stone. It was surmounted by a dome and adorned with arabesques of striking colours. The windows of the upper floor were plated with wood and framed in silver foil. Those of the lower floor were plated with wood and framed in gold. Djenné was then an attractive eleven gated city, encircled by a rampart, with solid, well designed buildings of two stories. Among its many marvels was the Great Mosque, which remains a masterpiece of the Sudanic style of architecture.

I have produced a good account of Songhai architecture in a book co authored by Siaf Millar and Saran Keita entitled *Everyday Life in an early West African Empire* (UK, SIVEN, 2013, pp.120-122, 138-149, 255-256).

Architecture of the Coastal States

The Yoruba Kingdom of Ife was located in southern Nigeria with Ile-Ife as its capital. Founded by the sixth century AD, by the twelfth century, the ruler lived in a palace made of enamelled brick and decorated with porcelain tiles. Ife's buildings were examples of impluvium architecture

Figure 13. One of the very many rooms inside the King's Court in Great Benin.

showing some similarities to the ancient city of Pompeii. Impluvium structures have four houses or sets of rooms at right angles to each other grouped around a single shared courtyard. The city had paved courtyards and public places decorated with American corncobs.

Susan Denyer detects a typical plan for Yoruba towns that echo the examples set by Ile-Ife and also Old Oyo. They had walls 4.5 metres high and had ditches cut around them. Ile-Ife had two concentric walls with ditches. Old Oyo was surrounded by a 25 km wall. At the centre of the city where two major roads intersected, lay the royal palace, itself enclosed by a clay wall, and next to it, the principal market. Another prominent feature was the temple or grove. The minor roads were divided into 'quarters' under the leadership of key dignitaries who exercised power and responsibility over the different heads of households. These 'quarters' were arranged around the royal palace in a satellite formation. The Yoruba palaces could have anything up to a hundred enormous courtyards, each far larger than that of an ordinary house. Their roofs were supported by elaborately carved wooden pillars inside and outside the building.

Great Benin (1460-1650) was located in southern Nigeria. The city houses were built in order, close to each other and lined the streets. As in Ife, the buildings were based on the impluvium idea, again showing some similarities to the ancient city of Pompeii. Each house had many rooms with verandas, and often of two stories, some approached by steps. The

Figure 14. Two story house in Kumasi as drawn by an English visitor in 1817.

walls were made of red clay. The roofs were made of banana leaves or palm. Moreover, all houses had wells supplying fresh water. The Kings Court was a city by itself and was comparable in size to whole European towns of that period. It could comfortably accommodate 15,000 people and had fluted walls and columns, some decorated with the famous Benin Bronze art. The city had perhaps 10,000 miles of walling and is reckoned by the *Guinness Book of Records* to have been the largest earthworks built by man in pre mechanical times. Benin City had a circumference of over 20 miles. It had 30 main roads, all 120 feet wide and very straight, laid out on a horizontal/vertical grid pattern. There were a large number of intersecting side streets.

In the late eighteenth and early nineteenth century, Kumasi, the capital of the Ashanti Empire, now in modern day Ghana, was an impressive city. The houses were typically of two stories each containing a toilet on the second floor in a room by itself. The Royal Palace was particularly impressive. Built by local masons of Fanti origins, the building had ten courtyards, with a flat roof and parapet, and contained a suite of apartments on the upper floor. A visitor to the palace remarked that they reminded him of Wardour Street in central London. Each room was a perfect Old Curiosity Shop.

CHAPTER 8: CRAFTS AND INDUSTRY

Glass

Glass was manufactured at Ile-Ife in the sixth century AD. There were glass windows in the Kumbi-Saleh Castle and in the Songhai city of Gao. In Benin, glass making had been organised into guilds. Production took place in workshops, equipped with dining halls and dormitories. Glass blowing was still practiced in Northern Nigeria in the early colonial period.

Ivory

Luxury tableware was made in Benin and in the Sierra Leone region in the fifteenth and sixteenth centuries. They made astonishing spoons, ladles and salt-cellars. Kongo also produced luxury items from ivory. Over 800 exquisite salt cellars of West African origin are in the European museum

Figure 15. Glass making in a Hausa workshop as sketched by a European visitor.

collections. During the Renaissance period, these pieces were much in demand at the European courts.

Textiles and Leather

Cotton cloth was mass produced by the Yorubas. It was also mass produced in thirteenth century Mali, sixteenth century Songhai, and nineteenth century Kano. African cotton products were superior to those from Manchester. In some workshops, master tailors employed up to 100 apprentices. Silk garments were made in fourteenth century Yorubaland, and fourteenth century Hausaland. In Kongo, fabrics named as 'satin', 'taffeta', 'velvet' and 'brocade' were manufactured. Some Kongolese textiles were considered better than those produced in Italy at the time.

Tanneries in Ancient Ghana and in Hausaland made leather goods. In the nineteenth century, the Hausas made leather sandals, bookcases, boots, and pillows. They exported a massive 10 million pairs of sandals each year to North Africa.

Soap

Soap was produced in many parts of West Africa made from palm oil. Historical records attest to people using soap in the Songhai and the Nigeria regions. West Africans produced soap on such a large scale that Portugal attempted to restrict the sale of West African soap to protect its own soap industry.

Agriculture

Tropical agriculture was well advanced. Farmers practiced the manuring of fields and crop rotation as standard. Unfortunately, this was a consideration for why Africans were captured by European enslavers to work in the Americas. They were skilled in tropical agriculture and this was useful to the enslavers.

CONCLUSION

West Africa lost a great deal from European predator activities of the last 500 years, with the destruction of societies and the capture and deportation of millions of people. The great historian, Professor John Henrik Clarke, suggested that one reason for the enslavement of Africans was the need on the American plantations for skilled farmers who could do tropical agriculture. I add that the African invention of the smallpox vaccine was also a contributory factor since Africans could withstand many of the European diseases. Whichever be the case, Professor Clarke has actually opened up a brand-new area of research.

In other words: What skills did the enslaved Africans bring with them to the Americas?

A team of scholars led by Professor Rodney Thebe Medupe, a South African astrophysicist, have analysed the scientific content of some of the surviving Timbuktu manuscripts. So far, their findings on Timbuktu astronomy have appeared in books, articles and a documentary. The team plan to repeat the exercise but with other Timbuktu manuscripts, representing the other sciences studied at Timbuktu. Curtis Abraham reported on this in *New Scientist*. He names the Timbuktu sciences they plan to cover in the near future:

'With barely a dent made in the Timbuktu manuscripts, the team are in a race against time. Over the centuries, the documents have been subjected to the ravages of temperature fluctuations, humidity, dust and grit, and many of the texts, written on delicate paper, are beginning to disintegrate. While conservationists race to save the manuscripts, Medupe's team plans to expand the project next year to cover botany, medicine, biology, chemistry, mathematics and climatology.'

It would be interesting to research how much of this was brought to the Americas by enslaved Africans.

SOURCES OF INFORMATION

Preface and Introduction

Garba Ashiwaju ed., *Cities of the Savannah,* Nigeria, Nigeria Magazine, no date given, p.41

Benaebi Benatari, *The Document of African Civilisation,* UK, Unpublished Paper, 1995, p.16

Kathy Brewis, *Writings in the Sand,* in *The Sunday Times Magazine,* UK, 28 January 2001, pp.32-35

Basil Davidson ed., *African Civilization Revisited,* US, Africa World Press, 1991, pp.31-32

P. Diagne, *History and Linguistics* in *UNESCO General History of Africa, Volume 1,* edited by J. Ki-Zerbo, UK, Heinemann, 1981, pp.250-252

Cheikh Anta Diop, *Precolonial Black Africa,* US, Lawrence Hill, 1987, pp.188-189

J. C. DeGraft-Johnson, *African Glory,* UK, Watts & Co., 1954, p.107

John O. Hunwick & Alida Jay Boye, *The Hidden Treasures of Timbuktu: Historic City of Islamic Africa,* UK, Thames & Hudson, 2008, pp.95-97

Lady Lugard, *A Tropical Dependency,* UK, James Nisbet & Co., 1906, pp.96 and 206-207

Saki Mafundikwa, *Afrikan Alphabets,* US, Mark Batty, 2004, pp.118-121, also 63-117

Momolu Massaquoi, *The Vai people and their syllabic writing* in *Journal of the African Society, Volume X, Number XL,* July 1911, pp.459-466

Chris Rainier, *Reclaiming the Ancient Manuscripts of Timbuktu,* in *National Geographic,* 27 May 2003

Ivan Van Sertima, *Blacks in Science: Ancient and Modern,* US, Transaction Publishers, 1983, pp.7-8, 24-26 and 197-214

Chancellor Williams, *The Destruction of Black Civilization,* US, Third World Press, 1987, pp.205-208

Claudia Zaslavsky, *Africa Counts,* US, Lawrence Hill, 1973, pp.138-151

Chapter 1: Mathematics

Curtis Abraham, *Stars of the Sahara,* in *New Scientist,* Issue 2617, 15 August 2007, pp.39-41

Ron Eglash, *African Fractals,* US, Rutgers University Press, 1999, pp.20-33

Charles S. Finch, *The Star of Deep Beginnings,* US, Khenti, 1998, pp.91-94

Henry Louis Gates, *Into Africa,* Television Series Part 5, *The Road To Timbuktu,* UK, BBC Television, 1999

John O. Hunwick & Alida Jay Boye, *The Hidden Treasures of Timbuktu: Historic City of Islamic Africa,* UK, Thames & Hudson, 2008, p.90

Karen E. Lange, *Djénné: West Africa's Eternal City,* in *National Geographic,* US, June 2001, p.110

Beatrice Lumpkin, *African & African-American Contributions to Mathematics,* US, Portland Public Schools, 1987, pp.40-41

Théophile Obenga, *African Philosophy: The Pharaonic Period,* Senegal, Per Ankh, 2004, pp.470-473

Claudia Zaslavsky, *Africa Counts,* US, Lawrence Hill, 1973, pp.105-107, 137-151, 190-193, 204-210, 213-218

Chapter 2: Astronomy and Physics

Curtis Abraham, *Stars of the Sahara*, in *New Scientist*, Issue 2617, 15 August 2007, pp.39-41

Hunter Havelin Adams III, *African & African-American Contributions to Science and Technology*, US, Portland Public Schools, 1987, p.60

Hunter Havelin Adams III, *African Observers of the Universe: The Sirius Question* in *Blacks in Science: Ancient and Modern*, edited by Ivan Van Sertima, US, Transaction Publishers, 1983, pp.27-46

Hunter Havelin Adams III, *New Light on the Dogon and Sirius*, in *Blacks in Science: Ancient and Modern*, edited by Ivan Van Sertima, US, Transaction Publishers, 1983, pp.47-50

Charles S. Finch, *The Star of Deep Beginnings*, US, Khenti, 1998, pp.235-260

Marcel Griaule & Germaine Dieterlen, *The Pale Fox*, US, Continuum Foundation, 1986, pp.193-194, 201, 423, 445 and 505

Sharron Hawkes (producer), *The Ancient Astronomers of Timbuktu*, DVD, 2009

Michael Palin, *Sahara*, Television Series Part 3: *Absolute Desert*, UK, BBC Worldwide Limited, 2002

Chapter 3: How deep did Dogon Knowledge go?

Hunter Havelin Adams III, *African Observers of the Universe: The Sirius Question*, in *Blacks in Science*, edited by Ivan Van Sertima, US, Transaction Publishers, 1983, pp.32 and 37

Marcel Griaule, *Conversations with Ogotemmeli*, UK, Oxford University Press, 1965, p.19

Marcel Griaule & Germaine Dieterlen, *The Dogon*, in *African Worlds*, edited by Daryll Forde, UK, Oxford University Press, 1954, p.83

Laird Scranton is in John Anthony West, *Magical Egypt,* Episode 8 *Cosmology* (television programme), US, 12 June 2003

Laird Scranton, *The Science of the Dogon,* US, Inner Traditions, 2006, pp.15-16, 21-29, 40-52, 66-78, 110-115

Chapter 4: Metallurgy

Fred Anozie, *Metal Technology in Precolonial Nigeria,* in *African Systems of Art, Science and Technology,* edited by Gloria Thomas-Emeagwali, UK, Karnak House, 1993, pp.83 and 89

Georges Balandier, *Daily Life in the Kingdom of Kongo,* UK, George Allen and Unwin, 1968, pp.112-113

Benaebi Benatari, *The Document of African Civilisation,* UK, Unpublished Paper, 1995, pp.18-19

Cheikh Anta Diop, *Precolonial Black Africa,* US, Lawrence Hill, 1987, pp.116-117 and 204

Ekpo Eyo and Frank Willett, *Treasures of Ancient Nigeria,* UK, William Collins & Sons, 1980, pp.148-149

Charles S. Finch, *The Star of Deep Beginnings,* US, Khenti, 1998, pp.32-33, 43, 45-47, 48, 52-53, colour plates 3 and 4

Lady Lugard, *A Tropical Dependency,* UK, James Nisbet & Co., 1906, pp.99, 112 and 208

Laure Mayer, *Black Africa: Masks, Sculpture, Jewelry,* France, Éditions Pierre Terrail, 1992, p.179

Sir Herbert Richmond Palmer, *The Bornu Sahara and Sudan,* UK, John Murray, 1936, frontispiece

Amon Sakaana & Adetokunbo Pearse, *Towards the Decolonization of the British Educational System,* UK, Karnak House, 1986, p.114

Fari Supiya, *Afterword: Where From Here?* in *When We Ruled,* by Robin Walker, UK, Every Generation Media, 2006, pp.654-658

Robin Walker, *Before The Slave Trade,* UK, Black History Studies, 2008, pp.6-7

Chapter 5: Medicine and Surgery

Benaebi Benatari, *The Document of African Civilisation,* UK, Unpublished Paper, 1995, p.19

Basil Davidson, *African Kingdoms,* Netherlands, Time-Life Books, 1967, p.85

Cheikh Anta Diop, *Precolonial Black Africa,* US, Lawrence Hill, 1987, pp.205-206 and 227

Charles S. Finch, *Africa and the Birth of Science and Technology,* US, Khenti, 1992, pp.26-28

Charles S. Finch, *The African Background of Medical Science,* in *Blacks in Science: Ancient and Modern,* edited by Ivan Van Sertima, US, Transaction Publishers, 1983, p.150

Aminatta Forma (presenter), *The Lost Libraries of Timbuktu, Television Programme,* UK, BBC Television, 2009

Eugenia Herbert, *Smallpox Inoculation in Africa* in *Journal of African History, Volume 16: No. 4,* UK, Cambridge University Press, 1975, pp.539-559

Time-Life Books, *Africa's Glorious Legacy,* US, Time-Life Books Inc., 1994, p.85

Chapter 6: Boat building and Navigation

Cheikh Anta Diop, *Precolonial Black Africa,* US, Lawrence Hill, 1987, pp.208-210

Charles S. Finch, *The Star of Deep Beginnings,* US, Khenti, 1998, pp.221-224

Leo Frobenius, *The Voice of Africa: Volume I,* UK, Hutchinson & Co., 1913, p.348

Harold G. Lawrence, *Mandinga Voyages across the Atlantic,* in *African Presence in Early America,* edited by Ivan Van Sertima, US, Transaction Publishers, 1992, pp.169-214

Ivan Van Sertima, *Early America Revisited,* US, Transaction Publishers, 1992, pp.1-28

Chapter 7: Architecture

Benaebi Benatari, *The Document of African Civilisation,* UK, Unpublished Paper, 1995, pp.15 and 17-18

Thomas Bowditch, *At Kumasi,* in *African Civilization Revisited,* edited by Basil Davidson, US, Africa World Press, 1991, p.385

Cheikh Anta Diop, *Precolonial Black Africa,* US, Lawrence Hill, 1987, pp.83-84 and 199-203

Nnamdi Elleh, *African Architecture: Evolution and Transformation,* US, McGraw Hill, 1997, pp.25 and 306-309

Norris & Ross McWhirter, *Guinness Book of Records,* 21st Edition, UK, Guinness Superlatives Limited, October 1974, p.129

H. Ling Roth, *Great Benin: Its Customs, Art and Horrors,* UK, F. King and Sons, 1903, pp.160-161

Reade, *The Palace, Kumasi, 1874* in *Pageant of Ghana,* edited by Freda Wolfson, UK, Oxford University Press, 1958, pp.161-162

Chapter 8: Crafts and Industry

Benaebi Benatari, *The Document of African Civilisation,* UK, Unpublished Paper, 1995, pp.16 and 20

Cheikh Anta Diop, *Precolonial Black Africa,* US, Lawrence Hill, 1987, pp.205-207

Titi Euba, *Dress,* in *The Living Culture of Nigeria,* edited by Saburi O. Biobaku, Nigeria, Thomas Nelson & Sons, 1976, p.29

John G. Jackson, *Introduction to African Civilizations,* US, Citadel Press, 1970, pp.207, 211-212 and 291

Lady Lugard, *A Tropical Dependency,* UK, James Nisbet & Co., 1906, p.207

Laure Mayer, *Art and Craft in Africa,* France, Terrail, 1994, pp.60-61

Conclusion

Curtis Abraham, *Stars of the Sahara,* in *New Scientist,* Issue 2617, 15 August 2007, pp.39-41

Blacks and Science Volume One

Ancient Egyptian Contributions to Science and Technology

AND

The Mysterious Sciences of the Great Pyramid

Robin Walker

Also available in this series.

PART TWO

INTELLECTUAL LIFE AND LEGACY OF TIMBUKTU

PREFACE

The city of Timbuktu has an important place in the history of the African people. Its intellectual tradition is well known and widely praised.

However, all of the important Black scholars have claimed that its intellectual heritage was destroyed in the sixteenth century by Arab and European invaders from Morocco. For example, Professor Chancellor Williams, in *The Destruction of Black Civilization* (US, Third World Press, 1987, p.207), claimed that: 'In the Muslim destruction of the Songhay empire, the main centres of learning with all of their precious libraries and original manuscripts were destroyed first.'

He was not alone in this view. Professor Cheikh Anta Diop, in *Precolonial Black Africa* (US, Lawrence Hill Books, 1987, p.182), advances almost the same theory. He laments on the loss of: 'the judicial and administrative archives: assistants of cadis [i.e. judges] kept minutes of the sessions. But tons of documents have disappeared.'

Professor Ivan Van Sertima, in *Blacks in Science* (US, Transaction Publishers, 1983, p.24) shared this opinion. He mentions how 'the razing of Timbuctoo' utterly destroyed African writings.

While the present author has the greatest of admiration and respect for these scholars, it is unfortunate that on THIS question the ideas of Williams, Diop and Van Sertima misled a generation of Black researchers. They misled a generation into believing that West Africa's intellectual heritage was mostly destroyed after the 1591 Arab/European invasion

The ideas of Williams and Diop have influenced an entire generation of Black scholars into believing that West Africa's intellectual heritage was mostly destroyed after the 1591 Arab/European invasion.

This section was written to disprove this idea. I can happily report that some of the West African intellectual heritage STILL EXISTS and the literature is STILL HELD by Black families and institutions. In addition, a number of scholars, notably from South Africa, have taken a scholarly interest in this heritage.

In writing this paper, I aim to accomplish three things. Firstly, I give an account of this amazing intellectual legacy. Secondly, I introduce the greatest scholar of the Timbuktu Age, Professor Ahmed Baba. Finally, I give an introduction to a sample of 40 old manuscripts held by an institution in Timbuktu, Mali, called the Ahmed Baba Institute. This sample is designed to give the readers some idea of the sort of books written, collected and studied by mediaeval West Africans.

INTRODUCTION

Until recently many writers on Africa claimed that African societies had no written traditions. With the rediscovery of old manuscript collections, some dating back to the seventh century AD, or earlier, this perception is beginning to change. Approximately 250,000 old manuscripts still survive in modern Ethiopia. Thousands of old documents belonging to the mediaeval Sudanese Empire of Makuria were unearthed at the Southern Egyptian site of Qasr Ibrim. They were written in eight different languages. Thousands of old manuscripts have survived in the West African cities of Chinguetti, Walata, Oudane, Kano and Agadez.

There are around 60 private libraries in Timbuktu still owned by Black families and institutions. These family collections have survived political turbulence throughout the region and the ravages of nature. However despite the many challenges posed by fire, floods, insects or pillaging, Hunwick and Boye, two leading authorities on Timbuktu manuscripts,

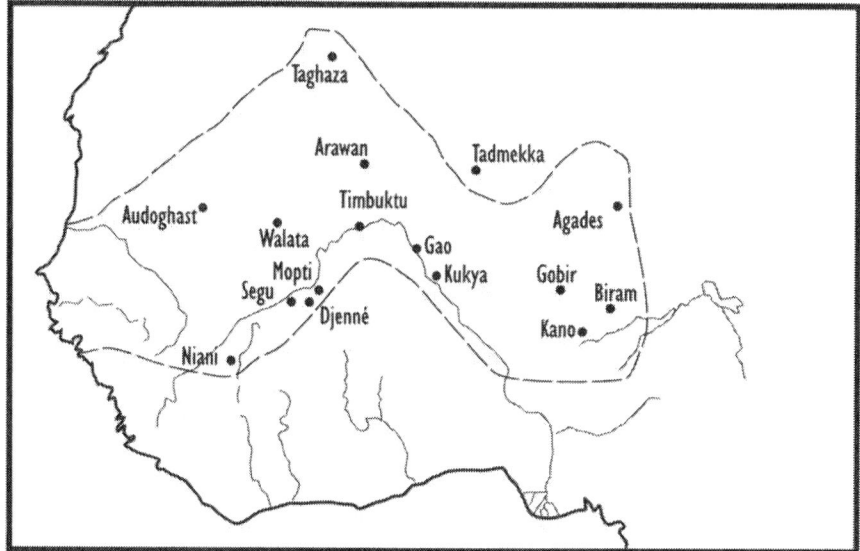

Figure 1. Map of the Songhai Empire showing the city of Timbuktu, now located in the modern West African nation of Mali. (Map: Kieron Vital).

estimate that 1 million manuscripts have survived from the northern fringes of Guinea and Ghana to the shores of the Mediterranean.

However, other sources give different estimates. *National Geographic* estimates that 700,000 manuscripts have survived in Timbuktu alone. Mary Minicka, the Head of Preservation at the Western Cape Archives in South Africa and a prominent figure in the preservation of the Timbuktu manuscripts, states that: 'Estimates of the number of manuscripts in Timbuktu vary, most starting at around a million. Other sources estimate that there are around five million manuscripts in Timbuktu and its immediate environs.' Incidentally, she also pointed out a little known fact that: 'mediaeval Europe ... ironically, created but a fraction of the volume of manuscripts produced by Islamic cultures.'

A good example is the Ahmed Baba Institute in Timbuktu. Established in 1970, this institution was named after Professor Ahmed Baba, a famous sixteenth and seventeenth century Timbuktu scholar. The Institute has nearly 30,000 manuscripts being studied, catalogued and preserved.

However during the period of French colonial domination, many manuscripts were seized and burned by the colonialists. Thus many families still refuse access to researchers for fear of a new era of pillaging repeating that of the colonial period. Other manuscripts were lost due to adverse climatic conditions. Following droughts, for example, many people buried their manuscripts and fled.

The manuscripts themselves range from tiny fragments to treaties of hundreds of pages. There are four types of surviving texts. There are the key texts of Islam, including Korans, collections of Hadiths, Sufi texts and devotional texts. There are works of the Maliki school of Islamic law. There are texts representative of the 'Islamic sciences,' including grammar, mathematics and astronomy. There are also original works from the region, including contracts, commentaries, historical chronicles, poetry, and marginal notes and jottings, which have proved to be a surprisingly fertile source of historical data.

The manuscripts themselves are of special importance to their owners for a number of reasons. For example, many people who are descended from the servile classes but claimed noble descent have been caught out by the manuscripts! Others relay information of unjust dealings of one family with another which happened a long time ago but have a bearing on today, such as land and property ownership.

So why wasn't this heritage recognised before? In 1894 France conquered Timbuktu. During the colonial period many of the owners of manuscripts hid them away or buried them. It is only within the last 30 years that the intellectual life of this region has revisited the sun. In addition, French was imposed as the main language of the region. This resulted in many manuscript owners losing the ability to read and interpret the manuscripts having lost the ability to read and write in the languages in which the manuscripts were originally written.

CHAPTER 1: ORIGIN AND EVOLUTION OF THE CITY OF TIMBUKTU

The great West African historian Abdurrahman Al-Sadi wrote *Tarikh al-Sudan* (i.e. *History of the Sudan,* which, in this context, means West Africa) in 1656. He wrote: 'I saw the ruin and collapse of the science of history. I observed that its gold and small change were both disappearing.' Al-Sadi was responsible for dividing the history of the West African desert region into the rise and fall of three great empires--Ancient Ghana, Mediaeval Mali and the Songhai Empire.

Ancient Ghana was the oldest of the three empires. At its height it ruled territories that we would now call Senegal, Gambia, Mauritania, Guinea and Mali. It was located between the two great waterways, the Senegal River and the Niger River.

Timbuktu was founded during the dominance of the Ghana Empire. Sanhaja desert nomads founded it in around 1100 AD. They had a tradition of camping near the Niger River in the dry season and taking their animals inland to graze during the rainy season. While the nomads were away, their belongings were entrusted to their slaves, one of whom was called Buktu. The campsite thus became known as Tim Buktu meaning 'well of Buktu'. What began as a semi-permanent nomadic settlement evolved into town and ultimately a city of permanent settlement. From 1100 to 1300, Timbuktu developed into a thriving commercial centre.

Located at a centre of commercial exchange between Saharan Africa, Tropical Africa and Mediterranean Africa, Timbuktu was a magnet that attracted men of learning and men of commerce. Timbuktu benefited from the gold trade coming from the southern reaches of West Africa. It also benefited from the salt trade coming from the Sahara. Approximately two thirds of the world's gold came from West Africa in the fourteenth century.

The products themselves included textiles, tea and tobacco. Based on the number of poems about tea found among the manuscripts of Timbuktu, this was clearly a special product. Tobacco use was even approved in a text by Timbuktu professor Ahmed Baba. His *On the Lawfulness of Tobacco Usage* claimed that tobacco was neither a narcotic nor an intoxicant! However, the

Figure 2. View of a trade caravan. From Major Felix Dubois, *Timbuctoo the Mysterious* (UK, William Heinemann, 1897, p.256).

most profitable trade item in Timbuktu was books. An old Timbuktu chronicle, *Tarikh al Fettash,* says that the King bought a great dictionary for the equivalent price of two horses. Buying books was considered a socially acceptable way of displaying wealth and a great source of prestige.

As the Ghanaian Empire declined, the Mali Empire took its place. The Mandingo speaking people, ruling from their capital city of Niani, founded this new empire. The Mali king Sundiata Keita conquered Ancient Ghana in 1240 AD. Two generations later Mansa Musa I built the Mali Kingdom into the Mali Empire. Islam became the dominant religion of the Malian cities and Arabic became the language of scholarship.

Arabic could be described as the 'Latin of Africa.' It was useful when communicating between the different peoples such as Bambara, Fulani, Hausa, Mossi, Songhai and Tuareg. Just as Latin in mediaeval Europe was associated with Christianity, Arabic in mediaeval Africa was associated with Islam. Just as Europeans adopted the Latin script to write their own languages, Africans used the Arabic script to write their own languages.

The BBC made a documentary series called *Millennium: One Thousand Years of History* shown in 1999. They opened the 14th century programme with the following disclosure: 'In the fourteenth century, the century of the scythe, natural disasters threaten civilisations with extinction. The Black Death kills more people in Europe, Asia and North Africa than any catastrophe has before. Civilisations, which avoid the plague, thrive. In West Africa the Empire of Mali becomes the richest in the world.'

What did they spend the money on? The Sankore University Mosque was built around 1300 AD with funding from a woman of the Aghlal, a religious

Tuareg ethnic group. Some writers give earlier dates. The Sankore Quarter in north-east Timbuktu became the dwelling place of the scholars and teachers. It was also where the first libraries were created. Scholars and kings acquired books during their travels. Books were also acquired from merchants coming from the north with books for sale. Mansa Musa I bought works on Maliki law. He also ordered the construction of the Great Mosque of Timbuktu in 1326.

There were a number of challenges to Malian hegemony, however. In 1343, the Mossi attacked Timbuktu. A source says: 'The Mossi sultan entered Timbuktu, and sacked and burned it killing many persons and looting it before returning to his land.' Timbuktu however recovered and the Malians continued to rule it for the next hundred years. However: 'The Tuaregs began to raid and cause havoc on all sides. The Malians, bewildered by their many depredations, refused to make a stand against them.' Mali lost control of Timbuktu in 1433.

The Songhai were once tributary to the Mali Empire but became independent as Mali declined. Sunni Ali Ber was the first great Songhai king. He conquered most of the Songhai Empire seizing Timbuktu in 1469. The chronicles say he 'perpetuated terrible wickedness in the city, putting it to flame, sacking it, and killing large numbers of people.' The gold traders feared Sunni Ali would take control over their goods and transactions so many started trading via Kano in Northern Nigeria. The scholars of Timbuktu experienced a major setback. Sunni Ali drove the Sanhaja out of Timbuktu and undertook a purge of the scholars. Many fled to Walata.

Subsequent rulers of the Askiya Dynasty adopted a gentler approach towards the scholars. They offered them cash and in-kind privileges especially during Ramadan. These included slaves, grants of land and privileges, and exemptions from taxation. This raises the interesting question: why were they offered slaves? Major Felix Dubois, author of the excellent *Timbuctoo the Mysterious,* says: 'To ensure them the tranquillity so necessary to a man of thought and letters, their affairs were managed and their properties cultivated by their slaves.'

Timbuktu benefited under the reign of the Askiya Dynasty. This is what that the *Tarikh al Fettash* says: 'One cannot count either the virtues or the qualities of [Askiya Muhammad I], such is his excellent politics, his kindness towards his subjects and his solicitude towards the poor. One cannot find his equal either among those who preceded him, nor those who followed. He had a great affection for the scholars, saints and men of

Figure 3. The Great Mosque in Timbuktu, 1326.

learning.' However, with Islam dominating the cities and traditional religions dominating the villages it is clear that the villagers did not necessarily benefit from the Askiya Dynasty.

Timbuktu eventually rose to intellectual dominance throughout the region. Walata 'where the holiest and most learned men resided' and Djenné were centres of Islamic scholarship in the early days. Djenné had a university which boasted of having thousands of teachers. There were reports of several different surgical operations successfully performed by their medical doctors such as eye cataract surgery. Timbuktu surpassed both of them after the year 1500.

The scholars and students came from the entire region including Saharan and Mediterranean Africa. There were scholarly connections between Timbuktu and Fez. North African and Andalusian scholars visited and settled in and around Timbuktu. In addition, connections were made with fellow scholars in Egypt and Mecca during pilgrimages.

What was life like in Timbuktu? According to the *Tarikh al Fettash:* 'Timbuktu has no equal among the cities of the blacks ... and was known for its solid institutions, political liberties, purity of morals, security of its people and their goods, compassion towards the poor and strangers, as well as courtesy and generosity towards students and scholars.'

According to Leo Africanus in *A History and Description of Africa,* c.1526: 'The people of Timbuktu have a light-hearted nature. It is their habit to wander into town at night between 10 pm and 1 am, playing instruments and dancing.'

He also wrote: 'There you will find many judges, professors and devout men, all handsomely maintained by the king, who holds scholars in much honour. There too they sell many handwritten north African books, and more profit is to be made there from the sale of books than from any other branch of trade.'

Timbuktu was also a religious city. A West African proverb says: 'Salt comes from the north, gold from the south and silver from the country of the white men, but the word of God and the treasures of wisdom are only to be found in Timbuktu.'

There is a local legend that 333 renowned saints as well as numerous lesser saints guard the city. Surrounding the city like a rampart are chapels where the saints were buried. According to the Sufis, a saint is a Muslim mystic, usually a scholar, who has achieved such closeness to God as to possess special powers. For example, we read: 'The very learned and pious sheikh, Abou Abdallah, had no property, and he bought slaves that he might give them their liberty. His house had no door, every one entered unannounced, and men came to see him from all parts and at all hours.'

CHAPTER 2: INTELLECTUAL LIFE OF TIMBUKTU

The Sankore University Mosque was the main teaching venue since many scholars lived in the Sankore Quarter. Classes were also taught at the Great Mosque and the Oratory of Sidi Yahya. Most of the teaching took place in the scholar's houses where each scholar had his own private library which he could consult when knotty points arose. Very often the student would study under six or seven different tutors, each having a different specialism. At the height of the Songhai Empire, Timbuktu had 25,000 students.

The students would pay the lecturers in money, clothing, cows, poultry, sheep, or services, depending on how well off the student's family was. According to the *Tarikh al Fettash,* Timbuktu had 26 textile factories where each master tailor employed 50 to 100 apprentices. Employment was restricted to students at a certain level of education. Working in the tailoring industry, secured the students an income enabling them to further their studies.

The teachers were experts in number of texts. This is not quite the same as being an expert in a particular subject. The traditional teaching method involved the lecturer dictating a text to the students. The students would write their own copies and would read back to the lecturer what they had written down. All the students would do the same. In this way, students would learn from each other's mistakes. Once the correct version had been written down, the lecturer would explain the technical intricacies of the text and engage in a high level of question and answer.

Treatises on pedagogy have survived among the manuscripts. Some books mention how to learn to read, how to improve memory, suggestions on what subjects should be taught, and the qualities of an ideal educator.

According to a Timbuktu manuscript, an ideal student is: 'Modest, courageous, patient and studious; he must listen carefully to his professor and have a solid understanding of his lessons before memorising them. The students must learn to debate among themselves to deepen their understanding of the material. They must always have a great respect and a profound love for their teacher, because these are the conditions for professional success.'

Figure 4. View of the Sankore University Mosque in Timbuktu. From Major Felix Dubois, *Timbuctoo the Mysterious* (UK, William Heinemann, 1897, p.279).

What did they study? From Professor Ahmed Baba's account, he studied Arabic grammar and syntax, astronomy, logic, rhetoric and prosody. Textbooks were purchased and copied on a number of subjects including astronomy, astrology, botany, dogma, geography, Islamic law, literary analysis, mathematics (including calculus and geometry), medicine, mysticism, morphology, music, rhetoric, philosophy, the occult sciences, and geomancy. The 'Greek' astronomer Ptolemy was a basic reference for Islamic astronomy. The Greek philosophers, Plato and Aristotle, were also common. The Greek physician Hippocrates was popular as well as the Persian medical scholar Avicenna.

Students received a traditional turban on their graduation. Following this, there were a number of career options. Some lecturers issued licences that authorised their best students to teach particular texts. Thus, some students became teachers and lecturers. The *ulama* or *savants* had a variety of roles in Songhai society. Some became judges, others became imams and some became teachers. The rural holy men became parish priests--attending to every part of the life cycle of their flock.

What was the quality of teaching in Timbuktu? The level of teaching was as high as in North Africa and the Middle East, some scholars say higher. One story is that of the celebrated professor from Hedjaz who is reported to have arrived in Timbuktu with the intention of teaching, but after talking to some of the students and seeing their level of learning, he was humbled and decided to become a student himself! Lady Lugard provided another picture of the quality of Timbuktu scholarship. She wrote: 'The appearance of comets, so amazing to Europe of the Middle Ages, is noted calmly, as a matter of scientific interest, at Timbuctoo. Earthquakes and eclipses excite no great surprise.'

Askiya Daud, the sixth Askiya, established public libraries and employed calligraphers to copy books for him. Some of these books were given as gifts to scholars.

The book copying industry was well structured and extensive. At the end of the book was stated the title, the author, the date of the manuscript copy, and the names of the scribes who copied it. Some books also named the proofreaders and the vocalisers (i.e. scholars who added vowels to Arabic). Oftentimes the manuscript mentioned for whom the manuscript was being copied, the monies involved, who provided the blank paper, and the dates of the beginning and ending of the copying of each volume. Many copyists wrote 140 lines of text per day while the proofreaders read 170 lines per day. One particular multi-volume text indicates that the proofreader was paid half a *mithqal* of gold per volume (i.e. 1.75-2.5 grams) while the copyist received one *mithqal* of gold (i.e. 3.5-5 grams).

CHAPTER 3: WHAT IS IN THE TIMBUKTU BOOKS?

The documents range from one-page fragments up to hundreds of pages--one example cited by Hunwick and Boye, in their masterly *The Hidden Treasures of Timbuktu,* was a letter of 482 pages. Most of the Timbuktu manuscripts included Korans, Koranic exegesis, collections of Hadiths, writings on Sufism, theology, law, and other closely related disciplines. There was also poetry in praise of the Prophet. By the fifteenth century, however, Timbuktu scholars were producing original works as well as compiling new derivations and commentaries on established texts.

Mary Minicka points out the social importance of each manuscript. In her own words: 'Like elsewhere, the way in which the manuscripts of Timbuktu were made, put together and disseminated, has the potential to help scholars understand how ideas were spread. We tend to forget that beautiful old books and manuscripts do not exist simply because medieval monks in France or Islamic scholars had time on their hands and needed a distracting hobby to occupy them during long winter evenings. The many processes and materials required to create manuscripts were part of, or were in themselves, a very tangible economic activity from which people derived a living (and in some cases considerable social status), one that linked papermakers, stationers, scribes, scholars, bookbinders, tanners, gilders and farmers in a wide socio-economic network. This means that the whole manuscript can be placed under scrutiny: leather, paper, textile, decoration--each aspect has the potential to contribute a fuller understanding of the context. Or, invariably, raises yet more questions.'

Professor H. C. Bredekamp tells us that the manuscripts show various styles of calligraphy, leather covers, and golden illuminations. The various types of calligraphy showed the regional variation named after the town or the locale in which these styles originated. Among the various types of scripts was the Sudani script typical of West Africa, the Suqi script typical of the markets, the Maghribi script typical across Northwest Africa, the Sahrawi script typical of the desert, and the Hausawi script typical of Hausaland, i.e. northern Nigeria. There are also manuscripts in Turkish that use the Eastern Arabic script.

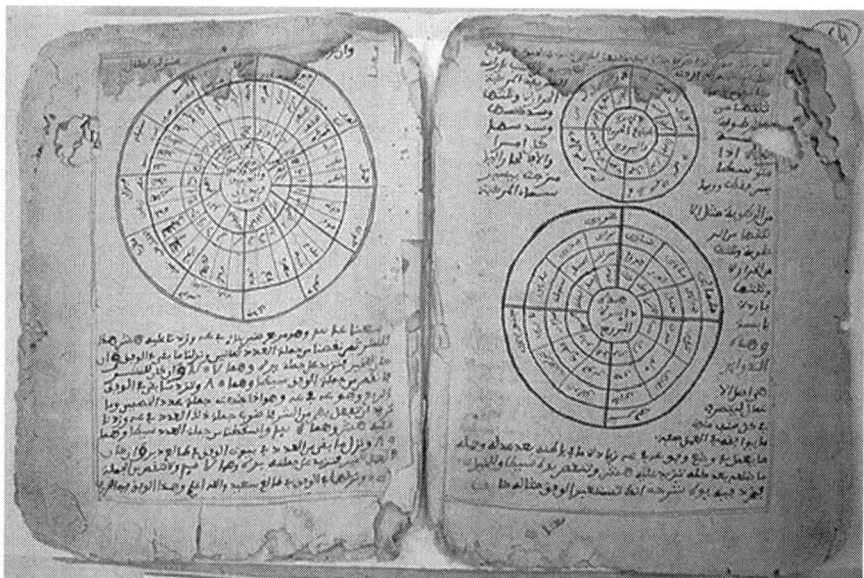

Figure 5. Old astronomical manuscript from the Mamma Haïdera Library in Timbuktu (Photo: Robert Goldwater).

Hunwick and Boye inform us that the commercial documents typically began with the phrase 'let all who read this document know.' This was followed by the names of the buyer and the seller, a detailed description of the product, a declaration of the legal validity of the sale, a confirmation that the purchaser paid the price in full, finally the name of the drafter and the date.

Legal documents also included a statement on the validity of the contract confirming the following: That the parties were legally competent, that they were free from restraint, that they were in full possession of their mental faculties, and that the transaction was lawful according to Islamic law. Legal documents typically ended with the phrase: 'Praise to God and blessings upon the Prophet.'

A related genre of manuscripts, are the fatwa texts. These documents contain the religious opinions of scholars on legal matters. The surviving libraries have substantial numbers of these texts. These documents typically consisted of a statement of the problem without naming names. Following this was a studied discussion based on well-known legal works and finally the document would end with the legal opinion of the scholar. Should the scholar not have copies of the standard legal works, he would have to consult with other scholars, borrow books from them, or have copies made. Thus a fatwa combines local history with the interpretation of multiple standard texts.

The reading and writing of poetry was important in these cultures. There were verses devoted to the Prophet, the adoration of a particular woman or a man, and even poems about tea! Poetry was written upon a person's death and read at their funeral. Even works on grammar and law were rewritten into verse to facilitate ease of learning!

Professor Shamil Jeppie raises some interesting questions that future scholarship may answer about the Timbuktu manuscripts that we cannot answer at present. He wrote: 'Was reading silent or collective? Was writing done privately at home or more publicly such as at a mosque? When were the ideal times for reading and writing? Finally, there are questions about the archive and library as presently constituted in Timbuktu, in relation for instance to the ways in which libraries were organized at various points in Timbuktu's manuscript age.'

There are a number of manuscripts written in Ajami. This is where the Arabic script has been used to write local languages. There are Ajami manuscripts in Songhai, Wolof, Hausa, Fulfulde and Tamasheq. These texts concerned botany, diplomatic correspondence, the occult sciences, poetry and traditional medicine.

Professor Ahmed Baba was the greatest of the African scholars. He complained to the Sultan of Morocco that his troops had stolen 1600 books from him and this was the smallest library of any of his friends. He wrote 70 works in Arabic, many on jurisprudence but some on grammar and syntax. Howard University professor Chancellor Williams says Baba was 'the greatest and most prolific African writer and scholar in the sixteenth century. Perhaps 'African' can be dropped here, for who else, Asian or European, authored a comprehensive dictionary and forty other [actually the figure was 70] works during this period?'

CHAPTER 4: PROFESSOR AHMED BABA AND FOUR OF HIS BOOKS

Professor Ahmed Baba was the greatest scholar of the golden age of Timbuktu. What follows in this chapter is largely based on the splendid research by Mahmoud Zouber, a former director of the Ahmed Baba Institute in Mali.

Ahmed Baba was born in Timbuktu on 26 October 1556. His older family members were scholars and judges. His father and paternal uncle directed his early education. They taught him the ability to read and memorise the Koran. Following this, he studied, over a period of 10 years, the classic texts of Islamic exegesis, law, traditions of the Prophet, grammar, theology, and mysticism with the great Professor Muhammad Baghayogho al-Wangari. Finally, he pursued studies with Ahmed bin Said and Qadi al-Aqib bin Muhammad Aqit, who were other Timbuktu intellectuals.

Unfortunately, a combined Arab and European army attacked Timbuktu in 1591 sent by Morocco. Ahmed Baba, then in his mid-30s, opposed the Moroccan conquest and became a leader of the opposition to it. In October 1593, the Moroccan Sultan ordered the arrest of the scholars which led to Professor Baba and all of his family being captured and sent in chains to Morocco. On his arrival in the city of Marrakech, he was placed under house arrest for two years.

However, he was released from house arrest on the condition that he remained in Marrakech. In that city he taught at the university mosque giving lectures in Maliki law, theology, rhetoric and grammar. In Morocco he wrote 29 works. Eventually, Professor Baba gained permission to leave Morocco and return home. He arrived in Timbuktu on 27 March 1607.

He continued teaching in Timbuktu until his death on 22 April 1627 where he wrote a number of fatwa texts.

He directly influenced three important scholars: Abdurrahman Al-Sadi, the great historian who wrote the *History of the Sudan,* Ahmed Ibn al-Qadi, the Moroccan historian and poet, and Abu al-Abbas al-Maqqari, the mufti and imam of the Qarawiyyin mosque in Fez.

Historians of our times have heaped praise on Baba. One good example is the African American historian, Professor John Henrik Clarke, who wrote: 'Ahmed Baba was the last Chancellor of the University of Sankore. He was one of the greatest African scholars of the late sixteenth century. His life is a brilliant example of the range and depth of West African intellectual activity before the colonial era. Ahmed Baba was the author of more than forty books; nearly every one of these books had a different theme.'

The *Jalb al-nima* was a 32 folio text completed on 12 October 1588. Professor Baba explains the reason for writing this book as follows. 'It is, to alert myself and to warn my compatriots and peers against frequenting the company of "oppressive rulers" that I have composed this work.' His aim was to warn scholars to uphold religious law rather than being courted and thus corrupted by the princes and kings whose interests may conflict with religious law. Baba's own forefathers were persecuted during the time of Sunni Ali. He himself suffered under the Moroccan occupation.

The book itself contains an analytical table, which is part of the preamble, four chapters, and a conclusion. The first three chapters discuss the opinions of Islamic authorities who share differing views on this question. In the fourth chapter, Baba gives his own position. He wrote: 'There is, in what we have said, enough proof to convince the scholars and all those who hope for the salvation of their souls and wish to escape peril, to stay away from oppressive rulers.'

The *Tufhat al-fudala* was completed on 11 July 1603. The book consists of a preamble, three chapters, and a conclusion. The first chapter is called The Virtues and Merits of the Ulama. The second chapter documents the importance of religious science over spiritual practice. The third chapter compares the relative merits of the scholars against the saints. In the conclusion, Baba puts forward his own opinion.

What were the issues at stake here? Baba writes: 'For some, the scholars are superior to the saints-sages, while for others, it is the latter who are superior.' The four founding fathers of the Islamic judicial schools (Malik, Abu Hanifa, al-Shafi'i and Ahmed bin Hanbal) were the first to argue for the superiority of scholars. Baba considers their arguments that the study of spiritual practice only benefits the individual saint but does not extent enough benefit to the community at large. On the other hand, the scholarly mystic al-Ghazali argued the superiority of the saints. Baba considers his argument and those who agree with him that there is a difference between interior sciences and exterior sciences. Pursuing the interior sciences embellishes the individual's soul with virtues. However, pursuing the exterior sciences tends to lead an individual away from the path of God.

Baba concludes that the scholars are superior but concedes that those who oppose this position have good arguments that have merit. In his own words: 'We tend towards the idea of the pre-eminence of the scholars, as proven by numerous *hadith* and *athars* as well as numerous traditions going back to the 'virtuous ancients'. But the scholars meant here are those who prove their piety and devotion and live in conformity with the teachings of the Qur'an and the Sunna, and not those who seek to derive from their science the immediate interests or a personal glory.'

The *Kifaya al-muhtaj* is a large 244 page document also completed on 11 July 1603. Considered Baba's most famous book, English speakers describe it as a *Biographical Dictionary*. Arranged in alphabetical order, the document presents biographical information of 662 principal scholars of the Maliki school who lived between the thirteenth and the seventeenth centuries. Baba details their origins, what is known of their character, their scholarship, their books, their teachers, their disciples and historical events that occurred during their lifetimes. The book mentions the schools and universities in the area, the books that we used for instruction, the large libraries, et cetera. Baba is careful to detail where his source material came from. He cites 40 books that he used as source material. Moreover he interviewed many of his contemporaries including his disciple Muhammad bin Yaqub al-Marrakushi. In short, the *Biographical Dictionary* is one of the main sources of the intellectual life of the Magreb until the end of the sixteenth century.

Major Felix Dubois says that this book 'had such a great success in both northern and negraic Africa that the author was obliged to publish a popular edition containing the principal biographies only.'

Finally, the *Mi'raj al-su'ud* (known to English speakers as *The Law of Slavery*) was completed on 9 February 1615. Apparently people from the city of Tuat in the far north of the Songhai Empire contacted Professor Baba to enquire on the legality of enslaved Africans passing through this city. Baba answered their questions methodically.

For instance, a question that was posed was: 'Can one, under the letter of the law, consider oneself as the legitimate owner of these individuals?' Baba replied that the internecine slave raids that produced this slave traffic defied the protective laws of jihad and therefore such commerce was forbidden. Moreover Baba addressed the idea, arguably derived from the *Talmud,* that Black people belonged to the 'cursed' race of Ham who were ordered to be the slaves of the descendants of Shem and Japheth. Baba suggested that this passage, and the interpretation given to it, was apocryphal. In any case, 'Supposing that [Ham] is the father of the people of the Bilad al-Sudan', wrote Baba, 'God is too merciful to make millions atone for the fault of one man.'

In addition Baba stresses the need to treat slaves with consideration adding that 'Your slaves are your brothers.' Moreover 'God orders that slaves must be treated with humanity, whether they are black or not; one must pity their sad luck, and spare them bad treatment, since just the fact of becoming the owner of another person bruises the heart, because servitude is inseparable from the idea of violence and domination, especially when it relates to a slave taken far away from his country.' However, despite this positive and nuanced position, Professor Baba did not condemn slavery unequivocally.

CHAPTER 5: A SAMPLE OF 40 TIMBUKTU MANUSCRIPTS

In 2008 the South African-Mali project produced an exhibition called *Timbuktu Script & Scholarship*. The exhibition was one of the outcomes of a project which was initiated in 2003 on African Day by President Thabo Mbeki of South Africa. President Mbeki himself suggested that one of the aims of the project was to conserve the important collection of manuscripts held at the Ahmed Baba Institute in Timbuktu and to build a new library and archives for the Ahmed Baba Institute.

The President of Mali, Amadou Toumani Touré, was the other key player in the project. In his view: "The erudition of these wise elders fostered the production of an original and varied body of important works in mathematics, esoteric arts and practices, medicine, poetry and music, as well as astronomy, and reflections on the resolution of community and ethnic conflicts."

In putting together the exhibition for South Africa, the scholars chose 40 manuscripts from the Ahmed Baba Institute of Timbuktu. Since a number of the manuscripts were in an extremely fragile condition, this helped to determine which ones could or could not withstand the journey to South Africa. The catalogue numbers given to each manuscript is the archive number used by the Ahmed Baba Institute.

Manuscript 776 is a copy of a sixteenth century work by the great Timbuktu professor Ahmed Baba. The paper praises the search for knowledge and the intrinsic worth of scholarship. It includes the famous saying that on the day of judgement the ink of the scholars will be measured against the blood of the martyrs and found to be weightier. Manuscript 3856 is a copy of an early eighteenth century book called *The joyous Companion of those whom I met of the Maghribi Men of Letters*. The book contains information, gossip, and anecdotes concerning a hundred major writers from Northwest Africa. The book also celebrates the value of literature and the beauty of calligraphy.

The exhibition contained a number of religious texts. Manuscript 1515 is a beautifully ornate eighteenth century copy of three chapters of the Koran (originally seventh century). Manuscript 16,077 is a very small twentieth century copy of the Koran written on European machine made paper.

Manuscript 3874 is a copy of a ninth century work on the Hadith by the central Asian scholar Muhammad bin Ismail al-Bhukari. The Hadith is the life and sayings of the Prophet. The owners of the manuscript have added extensive commentaries of their own in the margins. Manuscript 165 is a copy of the twelfth century work by a Maghribi scholar Qadi Iyad entitled *The Rights of the Prophet*. Recounting the life and high moral qualities of the Prophet in a poetic metre, the book details his marvels and miracles. It also includes the ancestry of the Prophet going back 21 generations. After the Koran, this was the second most popular book read in West Africa. It was customary to read the book aloud during Ramadan in Arabic and then immediately translate it into Songhai. Manuscript 20,529 is called *On the Merits of the Prophet Muhammad and his Companions*. The book demonstrates moral character by using the example of the Prophet and his four outstanding companions as worthy models to emulate. Finally, Manuscript 1085 is a copy of a theological text written in the early fifteenth century. Composed by Muhammad bin Abi Bakr bin Abd al-Aziz bin Jama'a, the book presents the varied opinions on fundamental theological issues held by different authorities on questions such as how should an individual interpret God's actions. This text was of great pedagogical value and was used widely in West African education.

Other texts addressed the sciences. Some of these have impressive drawings and are composed in more than one colour. Manuscript 2163 is a copy of an eleventh century Egyptian astronomical text. Containing tables, the text illustrate the changing position of the stars, constellations and the moon. Manuscript 3666 is a didactic poem on astronomy. The author discusses the transition of day into night, and mentions the eleventh century scholar Ibn al-Haytham al-Baghdadi. Of a slightly wider remit, Manuscript 4058 covers astronomy and geography. It contains a description of the lines of latitude, longitude, and the dimensions of this planet. The author also considers the movement of the constellations and the succession of day and night. Finally, Manuscript 4056 is a physics paper on optics. The paper describes the properties and behaviour of light, and the interaction of light with matter.

Other texts addressed esoteric and the occult sciences. Manuscript 5235 is a commentary by Muhammad Abdullah bin Umar on the ideas of a sixteenth century Moroccan astrologer al-Fasi. Manuscript 6230 is a treatise on geomancy, which means divination by interpreting markings on the ground. Abd Allah Muhammad al-Zanati wrote the book to apply geomancy to military conflicts. He wanted to be able to predict who would

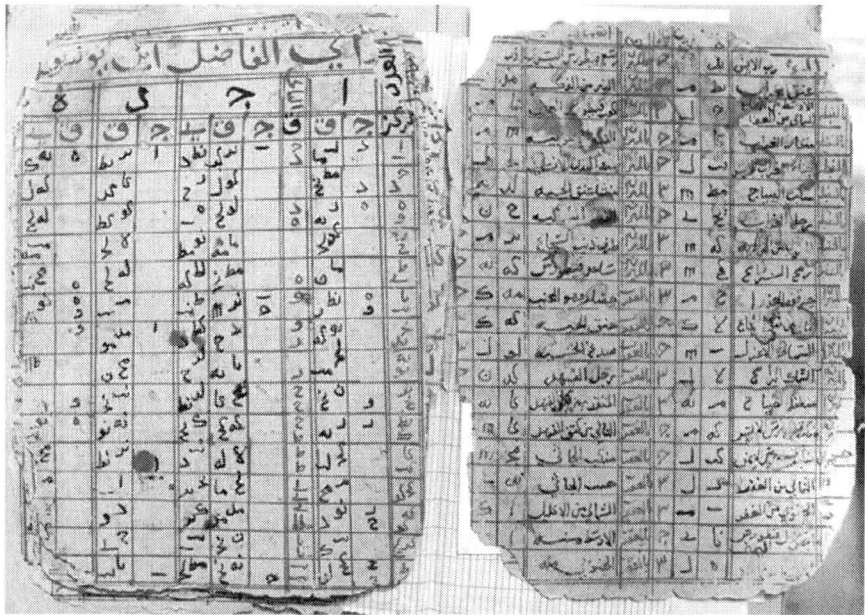

Figure 6. Manuscript 2163 from the Ahmed Baba Institute on astronomy (Photo: public domain).

win a battle, what the winners would gain, predict where the enemy would be, and predict whether the winning army would return without loss. Manuscript 8898 is a commentary on an earlier book by a twelfth century scholar called Abu Hamid al-Ghazali. The manuscript is called *The lofty tower in the elucidation of the Ghazalian triangle.* Among the subjects mentioned in this paper are geomancy, astrology and numerology.

Of a diametrically opposite nature is Manuscript 2399, a strict religious text called *Begging the Help of God in extinguishing some of the Innovations that have been Ignited and reviving those dying Acts of the Prophetic Sunna.* Among the things that annoyed the author of this text, was the numerous mosques proliferating in a single village, women visiting cemeteries, people raising their voices when praying, people spitting in public, people blowing their noses in public, and people placing their shoes inside a mosque.

Manuscript 2309 contains numerous extracts in verse from an eleventh century work on medicine by the great Persian scholar Ibn Sina (also called Avicenna). Encyclopaedic in form, Ibn Sina gathered the known medical knowledge of his time and made his own advances in the link between physical and psychological health, and the spread of contagious diseases. This manuscript also contains other ideas by Ibn Sina from the treatment of broken bones, to keeping teeth clean, to healthy living. Manuscript 5292 concerns sexual intimacy between men and women and the treatment of sexual complaints. It also describes treatments for eye infections, headaches, infertility and even forgetfulness.

Some manuscripts were of interest due to the languages used or the language instruction of the texts. Manuscript 786 is a copy of the thirteenth century didactic poem by an Egyptian scholar called Ibn Malik. Called *Alfiyah ibn Malik,* the poem contains 1,000 couplets that cover Arabic vocabulary, and the rules of morphology and syntax. West African pedagogues used this text as their most important teaching tool to master Arabic. Pupils and students had to memorise this text before they were considered to have a proficient grasp of the language. Manuscript 2458 is a guide, written in verse, to learning the language of the Fulani. Manuscript 4849 is written in a local African language that contains Koranic verses to do good deeds and to observe Islamic etiquette. Finally, Manuscript 4011 is a poem of supplication to God that also seeks the intercession of the Prophet. Written in an Arabic dialect popular in northern Mauritania, the poem includes words from Tamasheq, the language of the desert nomads. The text also contains magic squares.

Manuscript 2145 is a copy of *On the Obligations of Princes.* Written in the fifteenth century by a renowned Algerian professor, Abd al-Karim al-Maghili, the book was commissioned by the great Hausa ruler Muhammadu Rumfa. The book is a guide that defines responsibilities and duties of a ruler and details the requirements of good governance.

Manuscript 681 is a copy of the *History of the Sudan,* the great chronicle of West African history. Written in 1656 by Abdurrahman Al-Sadi, a Timbuktu professor, the book narrates the origins and history of the Songhai Empire, the story of the city of Timbuktu, biographies of the saints and scholars of Timbuktu and Djenné, and the Moroccan destruction of the Empire. Incidentally, I wrote a book co authored by Siaf Millar and Saran Keita based on this document entitled *Everyday Life in an early West African Empire* (UK, SIVEN, 2013).

Manuscript 1759 is an 816 page copy of a seventeenth century commentary by Abu Abd Allah Fara on Maliki substantive law. The book covers the legal aspects of dietary laws and fasting, jihad, the penal code, ritual cleansing, almsgiving, marriage, and prayer. Manuscript 13,954 is another large work on Islamic jurisprudence. Amongst the many subjects

There is even more information on Timbuktu in this book available from
www.everydaylifeinanearlywestafricanempire.com

mentioned are the meanings and interpretations of holy war or jihad, and the legal and social consequences of enslavement.

On the subject of enslavement, Manuscript 5800 is a written correspondence that concerns the movements of an elderly woman slave and the writer's daughter. Manuscript 5520 is a one page late nineteenth century commercial transaction that involves the buying of male and female slaves, and also a quantity of salt.

Manuscript 4142 is a fatwa or legal opinion. It concerns a woman who complains about frequent abuse from her husband who wants to take her to a faraway land. The legal opinion explains that in principle harm should be prevented and thus the woman should not accompany her husband on this journey.

Manuscript 86 is a didactic poem entitled *The Key to the Wings of Desire on the Knowledge of Arithmetic*. An eighteenth century copy of an earlier work, the treatise shows how arithmetic should be used to calculate the division of a deceased person's estate among their heirs. Manuscript 4527 details the execution of a dead person's estate. Included in the inventory, was the dead person's house, books, garments, prayer beads, and a sword. The items were witnessed according to rules set out in the Koran.

A number of nineteenth century documents were chosen for the exhibition. Manuscript 1224 contains a didactic poem on the demerits of tobacco. Written between 1835 and 1852, the author concludes that tobacco is an intoxicant whose use should be banned. Manuscript 1 was a letter by a nineteenth century spiritual and political leader in Timbuktu called Shaykh Ahmad al-Bakkay. Written during a period of power struggles between different warlords of West Africa, the letter spells out the political differences between al-Bakkay and his adversary the ruler of Masina, al-Fallan Ahmed Ahmed. Manuscript 290 was composed by Al-Hajj Umar, a mystic and warrior, who founded the Tukulor state. Written to encourage reconciliation between the rulers of Hausaland and Borno, the essay drew on historic cases of reconciliation between warring Islamic parties. Umar held that it was more important to promote the common good than it was to advance individual political interests. Manuscript 940 is another nineteenth century work composed by Al-Hajj Umar. In this document, he reassured the people of the Fulani state of Masina that he only had a political problem with their leader, Ahmed Lobbo al-Masini, and not with them. Finally, Manuscript 5537 is a letter by a wealthy Timbuktu man given to a go-between. The recipient of the letter was to take the document to a goldsmith to commission different types of jewellery from 50 measures of gold.

The manuscript tradition continued into the twentieth century. Manuscript 3808 is an early twentieth century didactic poem that contains some of the teachings of a Sufi order called the Tijaniyya Sufi brotherhood. Manuscript 8855 is a 1926 piece of commercial correspondence of the sale of books and Korans. Other manuscripts mentioned earlier (Manuscripts 4527 and 16,077) were also of twentieth century origin.

Finally, some books travelled a long distance to get to Timbuktu, West Africa. Manuscript 1998 is a text of Turkish origin. It was probably brought to West Africa by a trader or a pilgrim. Manuscript 1999 is also of Turkish origin. Written in verses, the manuscript lists the 99 beautiful names of God.

EPILOGUE: THE END OF THE GOLDEN AGE OF TIMBUKTU

The Timbuktu Golden Age ended with the collapse of the Songhai Empire. This story begins in Morocco where Sultan Muhammad XI, also known as the Black Sultan, was dethroned in 1578. His Arab successor Sultan Al Mansur established a sinister alliance with Queen Elizabeth I of England. The English agreed to re-arm the Moroccan military. They provided the Moroccans with firearms and provided trained men skilled in the use of these weapons. The Arab European army invaded Songhai in 1591 and destroyed it. The invaders confiscated gold and resources. They enslaved the Songhai intelligentsia (including Professor Baba) and they attempted a confiscation of the archives and the literature.

With the Songhai Empire out of the way, two thirds of West Africa, that had previously been under a single authority, split into smaller and smaller political units. This made the region easy prey for European invaders and slave traders. A book culture continued even after this catastrophe, as demonstrated by the existence of the manuscript traditions lasting into the twentieth century, but the scholarly standards, however, underwent a decline.

Let me give the final word to Major Felix Dubois. He describes the decline in intellectual culture of Timbuktu following the collapse of the Songhai Empire. He wrote: 'I found and brought away from Timbuctoo other historical works composed at later date, upon the model of the *Tarik* [i.e. *History of the Sudan*]. One of them is called ... *Divan of Kings, a book on the Sultans of the Sudan* ... and narrates the events occurring between 1656 and 1747 ... Another book, on the contrary, has no title, but is known to us by the name of its author, Mouley Rhassoun ... Other documents and oral traditions permit us to reconstruct the order of dates and events, and, in its broad outlines at least, the whole of the Sudanese [i.e. West African] past is known to us. Although these two books are precious for their historical value, they entirely lack the literary merits which charm us in the *Tarik*. Intellectual decadence has made rapid strides since the eighteenth century ...'

BIBLIOGRAPHY

Introduction

John O. Hunwick and Alida Jay Boye, *The Hidden Treasures of Timbuktu: Historic City of Islamic Africa,* UK, Thames & Hudson, 2008, pp.9-16, 61-62

Mary Minicka, *CONSERVATION IN THE EXTREME: Preserving the manuscripts of Timbuktu,* in *A catalogue of selected manuscripts from the exhibition Timbuktu Script & Scholarship,* edited by Lalou Meltzer, Lindsay Hooper and Gerald Klinghardt, South Africa, Iziko, 2008, pp.34, 37

Robin Walker, *The Black Musical Tradition and Early Black Literature,* UK, Reklaw Education, 2015, p.61

Derek A. Welsby, *The Medieval Kingdoms of Nubia,* UK, The British Museum Press, 2002, pp.237-238, 241

Chapter 1

Daniel Chu and Elliot Skinner, *A Glorious Age in Africa,* US, Africa World Press, 1990, p.91

Cheikh Anta Diop, *Precolonial Black Africa,* US, Lawrence Hill Books, 1987, pp.177, 183

Major Felix Dubois, *Timbuctoo the Mysterious,* UK, William Heinemann, 1897, pp.277, 280-281

John O. Hunwick and Alida Jay Boye, *The Hidden Treasures of Timbuktu: Historic City of Islamic Africa,* UK, Thames & Hudson, 2008, pp.10, 15, 24, 33, 35, 45, 49-54, 81-83

Jeremy Isaacs (producer), *Millennium 1300-1400,* Television Series Part 4: *Century of the Scythe,* UK, BBC Television, 1999

Chapter 2

Major Felix Dubois, *Timbuctoo the Mysterious,* UK, William Heinemann, 1897, p.285

John O. Hunwick and Alida Jay Boye, *The Hidden Treasures of Timbuktu: Historic City of Islamic Africa,* UK, Thames & Hudson, 2008, pp.81-83, 87-90, 95-98

Lady Lugard, *A Tropical Dependency,* UK, James Nisbet and Sons, 1905, pp.206-207

Chapter 3

H. C. Jatti Bredekamp, *Foreword,* in *A catalogue of selected manuscripts from the exhibition Timbuktu Script & Scholarship,* edited by Lalou Meltzer, Lindsay Hooper and Gerald Klinghardt, South Africa, Iziko, 2008, p.10

John O. Hunwick and Alida Jay Boye, *The Hidden Treasures of Timbuktu: Historic City of Islamic Africa,* UK, Thames & Hudson, 2008, pp.93-96

Shamil Jeppie, *INTRODUCTION: Travelling Timbuktu books,* in *A catalogue of selected manuscripts from the exhibition Timbuktu Script & Scholarship,* edited by Lalou Meltzer, Lindsay Hooper and Gerald Klinghardt, South Africa, Iziko, 2008, pp.13, 14, 17, 18, 19

Mary Minicka, *CONSERVATION IN THE EXTREME: Preserving the manuscripts of Timbuktu,* in *A catalogue of selected manuscripts from the exhibition Timbuktu Script & Scholarship,* edited by Lalou Meltzer, Lindsay Hooper and Gerald Klinghardt, South Africa, Iziko, 2008, pp.34-35, 37

Chancellor Williams, *The Destruction of Black Civilization,* US, Third World Press, 1987, p.207

Chapter 4

John Henrik Clarke, *INTRODUCTION,* in *Introduction to African Civilizations,* by John G. Jackson, US, Citadel Press, 1970, p.21

Major Felix Dubois, *Timbuctoo the Mysterious,* UK, William Heinemann, 1897, p.308

Mahmoud Zouber, *AHMED BABA OF TIMBUKTU (1556-1627): Introduction to his life and works,* in *A catalogue of selected manuscripts from the exhibition Timbuktu Script & Scholarship,* edited by Lalou Meltzer, Lindsay Hooper and Gerald Klinghardt, South Africa, Iziko, 2008, pp.21-31

Chapter 5

Lalou Meltzer, Lindsay Hooper and Gerald Klinghardt editors, *A catalogue of selected manuscripts from the exhibition Timbuktu Script & Scholarship,* South Africa, Iziko, 2008, pp.7-9, 10, 13-14, 17, 45-136

Afterword

J. C. DeGraft-Johnson, *African Glory,* UK, Watts & Co., 1954, pp.111-119

Major Felix Dubois, *Timbuctoo the Mysterious,* UK, William Heinemann, 1897, pp.316-318

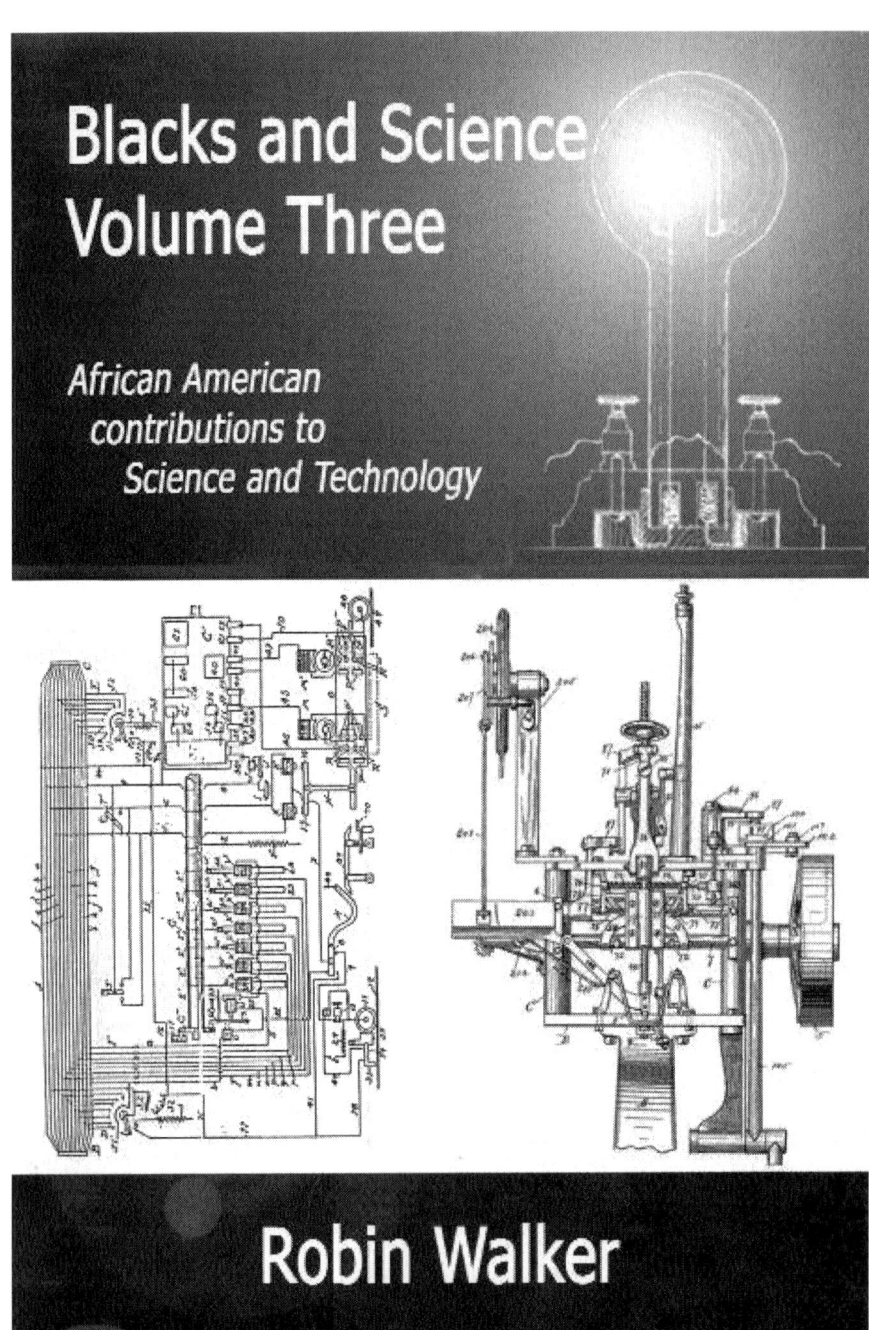

Also available in this series.

PART THREE

EAST AFRICAN CONTRIBUTIONS TO SCIENCE AND TECHNOLOGY

INTRODUCTION

A few years ago, BBC 4 present an interesting short film about multiplication in Ethiopia as part of a series about mathematics and number. Entitled *Go Forth and Multiply,* the film explained the millennia old system of multiplication used in Ethiopia by its traders and merchants. One of the products that the traders sold was coffee.

If an Ethiopian trader wanted to multiply 11 and 15, he would put the numbers into two columns. He would place the 11 in one column and he would place the 15 in the other column.

In the first column he would continually halve the number ignoring the fractions. Thus 11 halved is 5 (i.e. ignoring the fractions), halved again is 2, and halved again is 1. In the other column he would double the numbers. Thus 15 doubled is 30, doubled again is 60, and doubled again is 120. The two columns might look like this:

Halving column	Doubling column
11	15
5	30
2	60
1	120

There is a rule that one must IGNORE any even number(s) in the halving column AND the corresponding number(s) in the doubling column. Consequently, we shall ignore the 2 and the 60. Our table now looks like this.

Halving column	Doubling column
11	15
5	30
1	120

Finally we add up the numbers in the doubling column to produce our answer which is $15 + 30 + 120 = 165$.

The narrator commented that: "It seems unbelievable that a system can ignore fractions, even throw away parts of the calculation and still come up with the right answer."

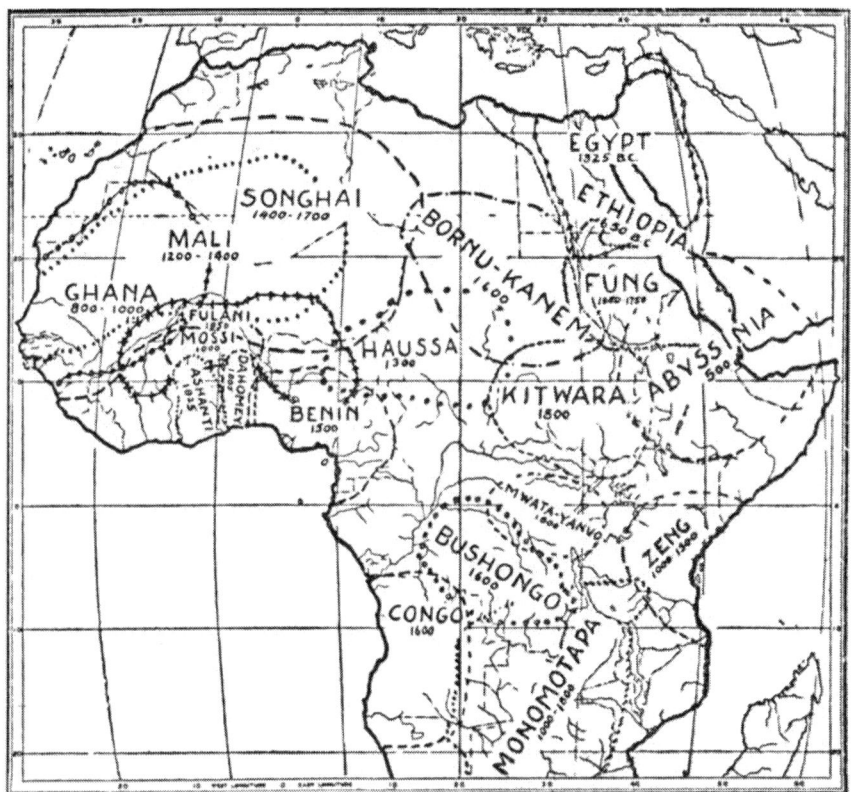

Figure 1. Map of the old African States by Professor W. E. B. Du Bois. Kush and Mediaeval Nubia are in the same place and correspond to his 'Ethiopia' and 'Fung'. His Empire of Abyssinia is clearly visible. The Swahili Confederation is his 'Zeng'. The Kingdom of Banyoro is south of his 'Kitwara' and the Empire of Munhumutapa has been spelled 'Monomotapa.' The Zulu Empire was to the south of 'Monomotapa.'

The underlying principle of this system is doubling which, at its core, is base 2 arithmetic. The narrator explained the significance of this: "It's a system that seems completely foreign to Western eyes but in fact we use it thousands of times a day because it's this system that powers today's computers."

In this section of the book, I will delve further into East African achievements. I will consider the contributions made to science and technology by the peoples of Ancient Kush, Mediaeval Nubia, Ancient Ethiopia (also called the Empire of Axum or the Empire of Abyssinia), the Swahili Confederation, the Kingdom of Banyoro (in Uganda), the Empire of Munhumutapa (centred on Great Zimbabwe), and the Zulu Empire (further south).

I will look at their contributions to the evolution of Mathematics, Architecture, Mining & Metallurgy, Astronomy, Medicine & Surgery, and Shipping & Navigation. As with previous sections of this book, my findings challenge and refute negative stereotypes about Africa.

CHAPTER 1: MATHEMATICS

Introduction

Professor Paulus Gerdes, a leading authority on African mathematics, reveals that traditional African know-how often demonstrates sophisticated geometrical knowledge. He demonstrates this by using examples of African wall decorations, rolled up mats, woven knots, woven pyramids, square mats, plaited mats, and plaited strips. For more information readers are referred to his *Geometry from Africa* (US, The Mathematical Association of America, 1999). To give an example, artisans from Mozambique traditionally used hexagonal weaving techniques to make hats, handbags, transportation baskets and fish traps. If the strips used for the craft making were of equal width, they were traditionally plaited at 60 degrees to each other. Other angles would have been used if the strips were of different widths. The 60 degree angles meant that the finished craft pieces contained equilateral triangles, rhombi, trapeziums, and regular hexagons.

Ethiopia

However, the most detailed knowledge we have of mathematics in early East Africa is from the research that Professor Otto Neugebauer conducted on fourteenth to nineteenth century Ethiopian manuscripts. This scholarly German found that Ethiopian monks and scholars traditionally kept 28 tables of 19 year calculations to reckon time in large blocks of 532 years (i.e. $28 \times 19 = 532$). Those tables contained calculations of calendrical parameters that ultimately allowed the Ethiopians to calculate Easter. The scholars made eight sets of calculations using algebra to solve this problem and thus compile these calendrical tables.

Let us suppose they wanted to know the date of Easter Sunday in Year x. First, the monks and scholars had to identify Year x correctly on the correct table out of the 28 tables. Second, they fed this information into a formula that enabled them to calculate the running total of differences between the 354 day lunar year and the 365 day solar year that applied to Year x. Third, they fed this information into another formula that enabled them to calculate the date of the Jewish New Year's Day. Fourth, they fed this information into another formula that allowed them to calculate the Jewish Passover. Fifth, they used yet another formula to calculate the day of the week of the Ethiopian New Year's Day. Sixth, they used this information to calculate the day of the week for the Jewish New Year's Day using simple arithmetic. Seven, they calculated the day of the week for Passover. Eight, they calculated Easter Sunday, again using simple arithmetic.

These calculations made extensive use of modulo arithmetic. Modulo arithmetic is where there is a limit on the highest number that can be calculated from a procedure. Once that number has been reached, we return to one and complete the calculation. For instance, the highest number on an analogue clock is 12. After this the next number is 1. So if a question required the calculation of 11 pm + 3 hours, the answer would be 2 am and NOT 14 pm! Mathematicians would pose this same question as: What is 11 + 3 modulo 12? This tells us that 12 is the highest possible number. The next number after 12 is 1, then 2, etcetera. If the question was posed as: What is 11 + 23 modulo 12? The answer cannot be 34 since the highest possible number is 12. The quickest way to arrive at an answer is to divide 34 by 12 and the answer is the remainder. 34 divided by 12 is 2, the remainder is 10. Thus the answer to 11 + 23 modulo 12 is 10. Since there are seven days in a week, 19 years in each of the 28 year tables, and 30 days in a 'full' lunar month, the Ethiopian scholars made extensive use of modulo 7, 19 and 30.

Some manuscripts discuss sexagesimal or base 60 fractions of the day. Others contain a concept called *kekros,* interpreted as 1/60. One particularly impressive use of base 60 appears in an Amharic manuscript. The manuscript gave the mean value of a synodic month as 29:31,50,7,57,30d. How should this be interpreted? This shows that the value was $29 + 31/60 + 50/60^2 + 7/60^3 + 57/60^4 + 30/60^5$ days in length. This is clearly a complex calculation.

I have written more information on Ethiopian mathematics in a book co authored by John Matthews entitled *African Mathematics: History, Textbook and Classroom Lessons* (UK, Reklaw Education, 2014, pp.48-61).

CHAPTER 2: ARCHITECTURE

The Empire of Kush

Kerma, the capital city of the Early Empire of Kush, was a particularly distinguished centre of architecture. The Empire of Kush was located in the same place as the modern Sudan and the southern portion of modern Egypt. Scholars divide the history of Kerma into the Ancient Period, the Middle Period and the Classic Period. These periods as a whole take us from the same time period as Dynasty VI Egypt to Dynasty XVIII Egypt. I controversially estimate the time period involved as *c.*4200 BC to 1601 BC.

Kerma, at the peak of its power was the largest city in Africa outside Egyptian territory, covering 65 acres. Surrounding the central parts of the city was a wall of massive size with a ditch in front of it. The walls were 30 feet high and made of mud bricks. They had rectangular towers that projected and also had four fortified gates.

Inside the city lay the gardens, the palace of the king, the houses of the nobility and the *deffufa,* a large white temple. It was 150 feet long, 75 feet wide, and a towering 60 feet tall. Its walls were 12 feet thick and were straight and even. There was also a second religious complex separated by a 16 foot wall. This complex consisted of bronze workshops, storerooms, housing for the priests, and also chapels.

Archaeologists working in the city have detected a large audience hall that probably dates from the Middle Period. This building was circular and may have been thatched. Also found were thousands of mud blanks that would have been used for making seals. This gives evidence that business transactions took place. There was also a great palace. It had an audience hall that included a throne on a raised platform. The king sat here and received delegations. Several large columns supported the roof and the building is believed to have been 25 feet high.

Kush flourished a second time between *c.*860 BC and 350 AD leaving behind a wealth of architectural evidence. There are at least 223 Kushite pyramids in the cities of Al Kurru, Nuri, Gebel Barkal and Meroë. They are generally 20 to 30 metres high and steep sided, sloping at around 70°. They were made of smaller blocks than their Egyptian counterparts. The

Figure 2. Temple of Amen at Naqa. 1-20 AD. (Photo: Louis Buckley of Black Nine Films.)

pyramids were used for royal burials and were entered by underground stairways on the eastern side. Meroë became the capital of the Kushite Empire from around 590 BC until about 350 AD, a period well attested by

Figure 3. Rams lining the avenue to the Temple of Amen at Naqa. 1-20 AD. (Photo: Louis Buckley of Black Nine Films.)

monuments. There are, for example, 84 pyramids in this city alone, many built with their own miniature temple. Moreover, there are ruins of a bath house sharing affinities with those of the Romans.

In Musawarat there is a very large and curious complex generally called the Great Enclosure. Dated at 220 BC, it has a series of walled enclosures and edifices that surround a central temple, itself built on a raised platform. Encircling the temple is a colonnade and outside of this is a series of ramps and corridors connecting the different parts of the building. Decorating the structure are elephant motifs.

The city of Naqa contains three important temples, the Temple of Amen, the Lion Temple, and the Kiosk. They date to between 1 AD and 20 AD. Kushite Pharaoh Natakamani and Queen Amanitore built the Temple of Amen and the Lion Temple. The Temple of Amen has a columned hall leading to an inner sanctuary as in Egyptian temples. In addition, there were 12 sculpted rams that lined the avenue to the entrance. The Lion Temple was dedicated to Apedemak, a local deity. It has a typical Egyptian-like pylon with the King and Queen depicted as conquerors bashing the heads of their enemies. The depiction of the Queen doing the same thing may represent a powerful role for the Queen or Queen Mother in the society or may even represent matriarchy. Behind the pylon is a one-room structure, a design unique to Kush. Finally, the Kiosk is a strange building that seems to have incorporated many cultural influences. There are arches, possibly reflecting Roman influence, and the capitals of the columns show traces of Greek influence. Some writers describe them as 'pseudo-Corinthian'. It is important to note, however, that there is no evidence that the Romans (or Greeks) built this temple. Many writers have hinted at this possibility, but in the absence of solid evidence, we must conclude that this is a Kushite monument built by Kushites.

Christian Nubia

The same Kushite region flourished a third time between the fourth century AD and the fourteenth or fifteenth centuries AD. For most of this period, the region consisted of two great Christian states--the Empire of Makuria to the north, and the Kingdom of Alwa to the south. Some scholars, such as the great Howard University social scientist, Chancellor Williams, regard this as the best period in the whole of Black history.

Archaeologists have found in Makuria and Alwa evidence of forts, castles, churches, monasteries, cathedrals, palaces, housing complexes with running water and water heating systems, toilets, and glass windows.

There were a number of fortified sites at Faras, Ikhmindi, Kalabsha, Sabaqura and Sheikh Daud. They had many features in common, both in their plan, and style of construction. Within the defences at Ikhmindi and Sheikh Daud, the layout of the buildings were remarkably regular and well planned. They had two roomed apartments that back onto the inner face of the defensive wall and were separated by a narrow street. The church occupied the central position. Other notable walled fortifications were at Bakhit, Diffar, Estabel, Jebel Deiga, Old Dongola, Selib and Sinada.

Faras was a much excavated city. It was found to have had defence walls that enclosed an area of 4.6 hectares. These walls were the largest building projects achieved in Medieval Nubia. The curtain wall was nearly 4m thick and 11.6m high. At the angles were substantial square external towers projecting 10m, while spaced at regular intervals along the curtain were slightly smaller towers. Two main gates survive in the centre of the south and west walls. Within these walls, there was a church of clay bricks constructed in the middle of the sixth century AD. Eventually, a cathedral

Figure 4. Three views of the mediaeval Serra East Central Domed Church. From Geoffrey S. Mileham, *Churches in Lower Nubia*, US, University of Philadelphia, 1910

was built on its site in 707 AD. The cathedral was a large five-aisle building covering 564 square metres and had Coptic and Greek inscriptions. In the tenth century AD the cathedral seems to have been damaged by fire. Two modern scholars, however, P. L. Shinnie and M. Shinnie, consider this building 'the superior of many buildings of medieval Africa and the Near East.' Also within the defensive circuit were three churches, two palatial structures, a monastery and an industrial complex that produced pottery. The two palaces date back to the seventh century AD and were linked by a narrow alleyway. They were certainly at least two storeys in height. Although built of mud brick, they had carved stone portals and the ground floor rooms were decorated with murals.

Qasr Ibrim was another important city. At one time, the hilltop contained churches, large areas of open piazza, a cemetery, and residences of important officials. An early visitor to the city wrote of its defensive wall and a 'large and beautiful church, finely planned and named after Our Lady the pure Virgin Mary. Above it is a high dome upon which rises a large cross.' This monument was probably built in the later half of the seventh century AD. It was a five-aisled basilica with a wide nave and apse. In size it measured 596 square metres. Beneath this building were crypts with barrel-vaults, 2m high, entered down two flights of stairs from the north and south outer aisles. The nave and aisles were paved with well-fitted stone slabs.

Arminna West and Debeira West were Nubian villages. Jakobielski, a Polish specialist in Christian archaeology, wrote that: 'Settlements investigated, such as Debeya [sic] West or Arminna, present a picture of a prosperous and at the same time surprisingly free and egalitarian society, where differences in social status were not reflected in material culture.' Specifically concerning the village of Debeira West, Professors Oliver and Fagan report that: 'The University of Ghana … [found that a]ll the buildings were of sun-dried brick, with vaulted ceilings. Two storeys were usual, with a stairway leading to the roof. The village shared a common sanitary and drainage system. There was a communal oil-press and an irrigation wheel.'

Old Dongola was the capital of the Empire of Makuria. From the seventh to ninth centuries AD, high status houses were built to the north of the ecclesiastical complex. Jakobielski provided further data on these houses: 'Further northwards extend a[n] … eighth to … ninth century housing complex. The houses discovered here differ in their hitherto unencountered spatial layout as well as their functional programme (water supply installation, bathroom with heating system) and interiors decorated with murals.'

Over the whole of this area churches and monasteries were found together with pottery kilns. Abu Salih wrote the following about the city: '[I]t is a large city on the banks of the blessed Nile, and contains many churches and large houses and wide streets. The king's house is lofty.'

Figure 5. Restored mediaeval Domed Church near Addendan. From Geoffrey S. Mileham, *Churches in Lower Nubia*, US, University of Philadelphia, 1910.

The Throne Hall of the Kings was probably built in the ninth or tenth centuries AD. It was constructed almost exclusively of clay bricks with walls 1.1m thick. The ground floor consisted of long and narrow barrel-vaulted rooms of a lofty height. On entering the building, the doorway led to a monumental staircase winding around a square newel. On the first floor was a square hall, surrounded by an arcaded loggia on three sides and with additional rooms to the west, flanking the stairway. The Throne Hall had a timber roof supported by four columns.

Another writer, Ibn el-Faqih, writing around 900 AD, describes the city as encircled by seven walls, the lower parts of which were made of stone. At a later date, the earliest houses were demolished and replaced by newer houses of two storeys or more. Many of these houses still survive to a height of 3.7m with large arched windows in the upper storey or storeys. A feature of these houses, which is common to the houses excavated beyond the defences, is the presence of a narrow toilet unit by the external wall at the end of one room.

Soba was the capital of the Kingdom of Alwa. Of this city, Ibn Selim, an early visitor described 'fine buildings and large monasteries, churches rich with gold and gardens: there is also a great suburb where many Muslims live.' Its Throne Hall was a clay brick building 46.1m by 18.6m. It had long narrow rooms at ground floor level. Like the rooms in the Throne Hall at Old Dongola, its function was probably to elevate the palatial apartments. Archaeology has recovered fragments of ceramic grilles for windows. The window glass panes were also found close by. Evidence of window glass was also found at the Makurian cities of Old Dongola and Hambukol.

Ethiopia

In Ethiopia, in the Tigre region, stands the ruined Temple of Almaqah. The pride of the city of Yeha, it is one of the oldest monuments in the country. Some think it was built before 500 BC. The Temple is a two-storey structure, raised on a stepped plinth. It is 25 metres long and rectangular in plan. The walls are of huge limestone blocks, finely dressed and polished with two small windows.

In and around Axum, another great city, there are over 50 stelae, many of them undecorated. Some are believed to be very old, but firm dates have not been established. Near to some of these obelisks, one kilometre from Axum on the road to the city of Gondar, is a massive building containing a drainage system with 'finely-mortared stone walls, deep foundations and an impressive throne room'. Ethiopian tradition establishes this building as the palace of Empress Makeda, the fabled Queen of Sheba (1005-955 BC). Tradition also establishes one of the obelisks, carved with four horizontal bands, each topped with a row of circles in relief, as the marker of the Queen's grave.

Axum itself has a series of seven giant stelae that date from perhaps 300 BC to 300 AD. They have details carved into them that represent windows and doorways of several storeys. The largest obelisk, now fallen, is in fact 'the largest monolith ever made anywhere in the world'. It is 108 feet long, weighs a staggering 500 tons, and represents a 13 storey building. The largest standing obelisk is 75 feet tall and represents a nine storey building.

In the twelfth and thirteenth centuries AD, Roha became the new capital of the Ethiopians. Conceived as a New Jerusalem by its founder, Emperor Lalibela (c.1150-1230), it contains 11 churches, all carved out of the rock of the mountains by hammer and chisel. All of the temples were carved to a depth of 11 metres or so below ground level. The largest is the House (or Church) of the Redeemer, a staggering 33.7 metres long, 23.7 metres wide and 11.5 metres deep. It is entirely surrounded by a forest of columns, all carved and sculpted. It is one of four churches that give the illusion of being

Figure 6. Temple of Yeha. Built before 500 BC. (Photo: Louis Buckley of Black Nine Films.)

freestanding in Roha (also called Lalibela), connected only by their bases to the rock from which they were hewn.

The House of Mary is another of the 'freestanding' churches. The Emperor considered it one of his favourites and the royal family used it to hold mass. It is 15 metres long, 11 metres wide and 10 metres deep. In its courtyard is a deep square baptismal pool.

Perhaps the most celebrated of the Lalibela churches is the House of Saint George. From the top of the monument, looking downwards, the church is in the shape of a concentric cross. It is more than 12 metres deep and its outer wall seem to indicate four storeys. Like the Temple of Almaqah, the church was built on a podium. The bottom rows of windows are similar in design to those seen on the old Axum monoliths. Other windows have pointed arches.

The architects of Lalibela seem to have absorbed or developed a wide range of styles. The House of Golgotha has pointed arch windows, with a tendrille-like tracery topped by a cross, similar to a Maltese cross. The House of Abba Libanos has plain pointed arch windows but also cross-shaped openings. The House of Mascal has Romanesque arches and windows of twinned crosses. The House of Mary has swastika-shaped windows.

Lalibela is not the only place to have such wonders. Peter Garlake, author of *Early Art and Architecture of Africa,* reports research that was conducted in the region in the early 1970's when: 'startling numbers of churches built in caves or partially or completely cut from the living rock were revealed not only in Tigre and Lalibela but as far south as Addis Ababa. Soon at least 1,500 were known. At least as many more probably await revelation to the outside world. A whole realm of architectural history awaits recording, study, and understanding.'

In the seventeenth century, Gondar, became the new capital. Emperor Fasilides founded the city and adorned it with huge gardens complete with pools and zoological collections. He built several schools and churches and aimed for the city to become a great place of commerce. Gondar has, however, been dubbed 'the Camelot of Africa' in reference to the fairytale castles that adorn its centre.

The oldest of the castles is said to have been constructed in around 1640 by an Indian architect. No such foreign claims have been made about the other buildings, however. These include the castle built during the time of Emperor Yohannes I (1667-1682) which functioned as a library. There is another famous castle, now derelict, built by Iyasu the Great (1682-1706). The Library was a two storey cuboidal building that had a parapeted flat roof and an outside staircase. The derelict building, sometimes called the Archive, in its time was ornamented with paintings, mirrors and ivory. Gold leaf and precious stones adorned its ceiling.

Figure 7. Archive (far left) and Library (centre) at Gondar. Both built by Emperor Yohannes I (1667-1682 AD). Castle (far right) built by Emperor Bakaffa (1721-1730 AD). (Photos: Louis Buckley, Black Nine Films.)

The East African Coast

The East Coast, from Somalia to Mozambique, has ruins of well over 50 towns and cities. They flourished from the ninth to the sixteenth centuries due to their role in the Indian Ocean trade. One of these cities was Kilwa, a former seaport on the coast of Tanzania. In the fourteenth century, Kilwa was a very fine place. One visitor described it as 'one of the most beautiful and well constructed cities in the world':

'Today [says a modern authority,] only a shabby village stands there. Yet beyond the village can still be found the walls and towers of ruined palaces and large houses and mosques, which is what the Moslems call their churches. A great palace [the Husuni Kubwa] has been dug out of the bushes that covered it for hundreds of years. It is a strange and beautiful ruin on a cliff over the Indian Ocean. Many other ruins stand nearby. But the strangest thing about Kilwa and the other towns nearby is that there is little to be found about them in the newer history books. Even when the cities are described, they are said to be not African, but the work of people from Arabia and Persia. History books saying this are out of date, and they are wrong.'

The other cities included the likes of Sinna, Zanzibar, Lamu, Mombasa, Gedi and Mogadishu. Their mosques were 'as grand as the mediaeval cathedrals of Europe'. The city of Lamu was apparently 'as sophisticated as mediaeval Venice'. Tradition has it that Lamu, the best preserved of the Swahili cities, was founded in 699 AD. Near its harbour are a number of splendid mansions, now deserted. They have reception rooms whose walls have tiered decorated niches. Also of interest is a fluted pillar tomb that may date back to the fifteenth century period. The city has over 20 mosques, all whitewashed, and also a few palaces.

In Kilwa the ruined mosque was once the largest of the Swahili temples. It was founded in the tenth or eleventh centuries AD, but it was enlarged in the thirteenth and fifteenth centuries. The north prayer hall was built first. It had a massive stone and concrete roof built on wooden rafters. Supporting the roof were a series of nine wooden pillars of polygonal shape. The domed extension, to the south, was built later. Between 1421 and 1430, it was rebuilt during the time of Sulaiman ibn Muhammad al-Malik al-Adil. Its roof is a complicated construction and has barrel vaults and domes over alternate bays. The interior has a forest of composite octagonal columns of rubble and cut stone, set in mortar. To the south of the mosque is a high wall that encloses an area for ablutions. It has water-tanks, a well and stone slabs--on which feet were washed and dried. In total, it was an admirable structure. One early Portuguese visitor compared its domed ceiling to that of the Great Mosque of Cordova in Spain.

There are other buildings of historical interest in Kilwa. Located east of the Husuni Kubwa is the Husuni Ndogo, a contemporaneous building raised by al-Malik al-Mansur. The structure has a massive wall enclosing a rectangular plan and covers an acre. At intervals along the walls and at the corners, are solid towers. They are polygonal in shape but circular at the base. The function of this great edifice is presently unknown but it may have been a mosque or even a market. South and west of the Great Mosque, lay the graveyard. This leads to a small domed fifteenth century temple. It is the best preserved and ornamented of the old structures. The customary vaults and domes ornament its roof, but an octagonal pillar, a most curious feature, surmounts the central dome. Islamic ware, consisting of small bowls, was set into the ceilings of the vaults. Above the *mihrab* were recesses for tiles and bowls. The eastern side of the building has a room that may have functioned as a Koran school.

Figure 8. Ruins of the Royal Palace of Gedi in Kenya. Thirteenth century. Photo: Robin Walker.

Gedi, near the coast of Kenya, is another ghost town. Its ruins, dating from the fourteenth or fifteenth centuries (the Kenyan museums say thirteenth), include the city walls, the palace, private houses, the Great Mosque, seven smaller mosques, and three pillar tombs. The walls are nine feet high and had at least three gates. Approaching the mosque was a washing pool for the believers to perform ablutions. It had a purifier made of limestone for recycling water. The houses had roofs of coral tiles covered in lime, walls of mortar and coral rag, and finely cut doorways of coral. The early houses were of one storey. They had a court, leading to the main room, and behind that was the private quarter. Also there, were smaller adjoining rooms, such as the bathroom, the toilet, bedroom, kitchen and storeroom. Later houses, from the fifteenth or sixteenth centuries, had upper floors. The royal palace had a layout similar to a large cluster of these houses, but with the addition of a reception hall. The palace contains evidence of bathrooms and indoor toilets. Finally, a part of this three-gated city had streets laid out on a north-south, east-west grid.

Southern Africa

In Southern Africa, there are at least 600 stone built ruins in the regions of Zimbabwe, Mozambique and South Africa. These ruins 'show today an extraordinary cultural past'. Most of them are said to date from the Middle Ages, but some authorities give much earlier dates for their construction. These structures are called Mazimbabwe in Shona, the Bantu language of the builders, and means great houses of stone. João de Barros, a Portuguese writer of the mid-sixteenth century, tells us 'Symbaoe' (more correctly 'Zimbabwe') in Shona 'signifies court'. Of the buildings themselves, Professor Diop informs us that:

'[T]hey are almost cyclopean structures, with walls several metres thick; five at the base, three at the top, and nine meters in height. Edifices of all types are to be found there from the royal palace, the temple, and the military fortification to the private villa of a notable. The walls are of granite masonry.'

The Great Zimbabwe was the largest of these ruins. It consists of 12 clusters of buildings, spread over three square miles. Its outer walls were made from 100,000 tons of granite bricks. In the fourteenth century, the city housed 18,000 people (some give higher figures), comparable in size to that of London of the same period. The buildings housed warehouses and shrines.

The walls of the central enclosure, popularly known as the 'Temple', reach 35 feet in height and 17 feet thick in places. They form an irregular ellipse with a maximum diameter of 292 feet and a circumference of 830 feet. The bricks are fashioned and arranged to hold together in regular courses without the use of mortar. The floors are of crushed granite and contain drains. One of the earliest visitors to the site, J. Theodore Bent, commented that: 'As a specim[e]n of the dry builder's art, it is without a parallel.' The tops of some walls have ornamental patterns, of which chevron and dentelle are the most common. For over 250 feet of its length, the chevron pattern ornaments the outer wall and is perfectly level. On the summit of the wall above the chevron work, stood a series of granite and soapstone monoliths and also a double row of small granite towers. Some of the other ruins show check, sloping block, and herringbone patterns. The North Entrance has steps that curve inwards in a semicircular fashion. This leads immediately inside to the great Parallel Passage, a distance of 220 feet.

Figure 9. Great Zimbabwe Temple. *c.*1335 AD.

Though succumbed to the passage of time, cottages once stood within and outside these walls for an area of three square miles. They were circular and thatched. Moreover, they had walls 12 to 18 inches thick and made of *daga,* a clay and gravel mixture. *Daga* was also used to make steps, fireplaces, chairs, bedsteads, and tables, all to a high level of smooth glazed finish. It was used to coat floors, again to a fine finish. Professor Finch notes that this must have had a 'dazzling' aesthetic effect.

The cottages were richly decorated with carved wooden beams and painted walls. Among the typical designs were paintings of animals, birds, people, and black and white squares. Some cottages had wooden doors, beautifully carved from selected timbers.

Perhaps the most well known part of the ruined complex is the Conical Tower. The Parallel Passage leads on to this curious edifice. It is 18 feet in diameter at the base and 30 feet high, though once higher. Next to the tower is a much smaller cone structure. The Conical Tower may symbolise a mound of grain and therefore reinforce the role of the king as provider for the people.

On a hill 350 feet above and overlooking the Temple is a castle, generally known as the 'Acropolis'. It has very thick walls, massive conical turrets, narrow entrances, and twisting passageways. The widths of the entrances vary from half a metre to just over a metre. The widths of the walls vary from 12 to 14 feet at the top to 19 to 22 feet thick at the base. The site may well have been chosen for security reasons, giving a panoramic view of the city and the surroundings. What is interesting here is that the hill contains huge stone boulders. The builders incorporated the boulders into the walls rather than clearing them.

CHAPTER 3: MINING AND METALLURGY

Kush

Archaeologists have found copper smelters at Buhen in northern Nubia. These smelters date back to the end of the Old Kingdom Period. According to Professor Finch, tuyères were placed through holes in the smelters where bellows were attached. By fanning the air, the smelters could reach temperatures of over 1083°C, the temperature needed to melt copper.

Bronze is an alloy of copper and tin. The addition of 4 to 15% of tin greatly improves the strength and hardness of the metal. In Kerma, the inhabitants produced bronze implements of exceptionally fine quality. As late as the Dynasty XXV period, when Kush ruled Egypt, the Kushites were still making high-quality bronze implements. Bronze artefacts continued to be made throughout the Meroitic era which takes us up to 350 AD.

The great archaeologist, Sir Flinders Petrie, found a cache of 23 tools from the Dynasty XXV period. Consisting of punches, chisels, files, rasps, adzes, etcetera, five of these pieces were analysed by scholars. They found that two of the five were actually made of low carbon steel. The carbon content amounted to no more than 0.1 or 0.2%. However, this was sufficient to produce a metal three times harder than iron.

Iron implements were discovered in Kushite graves dating back to around 750 BC. Archaeologists found an iron bangle, tweezers, an arrow head, a hook, a blade, an axe head, an unsocketed knife, and an adze. The city of Meroë was of course the centre of the Kushite iron industry. Archaeologists used to call Meroë 'the Birmingham of Africa.'

Gold and silver were among the royal metals of Kush. Gold was so commonplace that silver was often considered even more valuable than gold. Numerous examples of exquisite golden ornaments have come down to us including jewellery, inlay and sculpture.

Perhaps the most celebrated example was discovered in 1834 by an Italian grave robber. Destroying the Pyramid of Kentake Amanishakheto, the grave robber discovered superlative examples of Kushite gold work known as the Treasures of Amanishakheto. Other golden pieces recovered

Figure 10. Armlet from the Treasures of Amanishakheto. Gold and fused glass inlays. Height 3 cm. Width of each piece 9.2 cm. (Photo: Sven-Steffen Arndt.)

from Kush include ornate amulets, wadjet eyes, knives, decorated cylinder sheaths, tweezers, gold flower necklaces and earrings. The temples at Meroë and Musawarat had walls and statues covered with gold leaf.

Ethiopia

In the Empire of Axum, bronze was used alongside gold and silver to make coins. They also made colossal sculptures of bronze some of which were more than 15 feet in height. Equally skilled in gold, the Axumites casted large golden statues. What is remarkable, however, is the extent to which the Axumites entered the Steel Age. As Professor Finch points out, virtually all of their weapons were made of steel.

East Africa

Archaeologists have found iron smelters in East Africa going back before 600 BC. A number of examples were found in Rwanda, Burundi, Uganda, the Sudan, Kenya, Congo and Tanzania. Iron itself is derived from haematite ore. In certain parts of East Africa, surface haematite is relatively plentiful on certain hillsides. Metallurgists typically preheated the ore in very hot fires for approximately half an hour thus easing the separation of the iron from the ore before completing the main smelt. However, smelting required large quantities of charcoal which in practice meant that perhaps 15 medium-sized trees could end up being consumed in the process!

The early East Africans used two main types of smelters. One type was a large bowl set into the ground. The second type had a tall shaft perhaps 10 feet above ground. The shaft was often made of a special clay which contained quartz, mica and feldspar making the structure fireproof. It is likely that the tall furnace was used for the initial smelt and the bowl smelter was used to refine the metal produced from the tall furnace.

Archaeologists found a number of steel furnaces in the Lake Victoria region that dated back to about 500 AD. This finding is important because it indicated that certain peoples in what is now northern Tanzania (such as the Haya) were producing high carbon steel that was technically unsurpassed by anybody until the end of the 19th century. The archaeologists reconstructed these furnaces to show how they worked. They discovered that the ancient metallurgists worked at around 1450°C. They also found that in some parts of the combustion zone, they reached temperatures as high as 1820°C. This was the highest temperature achieved in a blast furnace anywhere before the end of the 19th century. This is significant as Professor Charles Finch explains:

'These astonishingly high temperatures explain a unique characteristic of Haya iron: contrary to bloom iron found throughout the world that forms by the sintering of fine solid particles, Haya iron forms by the precipitation of large crystals from the ore. The molten slag then undergoes a "carbon boil"--similar to the process in modern blast furnaces--resulting in a formation of two products pure iron and steel. This is an extraordinarily efficient way of producing iron since it requires less fuel than the standard Iron Age smelting techniques. As Nikolaas Van Der Merwe has pointed out, this methodology represents a significant technical innovation in steel manufacture that seems to have been unique to Africa. There are at least four places where crystalline steel was produced: Tanzania (Haya), Nigeria (Oyo), Ethiopia (Lake Tana), and Ghana, all presumably by similar methods. Thus, the induced draft furnace with a tall shaft plus preheating of bellows-driven air are two unique African inventions. The laborious processes of carburization, quenching, tempering, and hammering so characteristic of steel-making in other parts of the world seem to have been bypassed in a technical tour de force among those African peoples mastering the "Haya technique".'

The Tanzanian steel was traded by the Swahili in the Middle Ages to make the famous Damascus blades. The historian, Al Idrissi, in the *Book of Roger* (1153) makes special mention of what he calls 'superior iron'. This is a reference to the early Tanzanian high quality steel.

Southern Africa

Archaeologists beginning in 1902 began the rediscovery of Southern African gold mining in and around the Great Zimbabwe region. They found thousands of gold mines dug to an astonishing depth of 150 feet. The archaeologists estimated that the southern Africans dug 43,250,000 tons of ore. According to Professor Finch, this produces 700 tons of pure gold which equals $7.5 billion at 1998 gold prices.

One historian wrote: 'The bygone miners must have been industrious beyond belief, since they worked in rock so obdurate that the same sort of reef is nowadays blasted with dynamite, and yet they removed many million tones of ore. It is a practical testimony to their skill that the modern engineers follow to this day the lines of their ancient workings.'

Gold was used to make ornaments, jewellery and plate objects. All the goldsmiths art was practiced there including gold wire drawing, beating gold into thin sheets, plating iron and bronze with gold, and burnishing. Golden thread was woven into cloth and gold chain links were produced.

Figure 11. Old iron smelting furnace from the Zimbabwe region. From J. Theodore Bent, *The Ruined Cities of Mashonaland, 3rd Edition*, UK, Longmans, Green, and Co., 1902.

Gold was used to cover furniture to make figurine statuary, arrowheads and battleaxes.

Also in 1902, archaeologists found fifty pounds of iron hoes, a huge quantity of coiled wire of bronze, copper, and iron, some of which were twisted into bracelets. Also found were numerous copper ingots, copper jewellery, iron gongs and stone moulds for copper ingots. More recent archaeology has found abundant evidence of iron and copper mining shafts and furnaces dating from the eighth century AD.

CHAPTER 4: ASTRONOMY

Introduction

Astronomy has had a long history in early East (and Southern) Africa. Unfortunately some of what we know today about these early African endeavours is somewhat shadowy and vague.

Kush

Concerning astronomy in Ancient Kush, for example, Professor Finch reports that the Nile Valley Africans engaged in the calculations of lunar eclipses dating from the time when Kush ruled Egypt as Dynasty XXV. Lady Lugard tells us that on the base of one of the Kushite pyramids, a Zodiac was discovered. Professor Diop reports that Lepsius discovered in Meroë the foundation of an astronomical observatory. On the walls of the edifice was found a scene representing people operating an instrument resembling an astrolabe. He also found a series of numerical equations relating to astronomic events which occurred two centuries BC.

Christian Nubia

Another tantalising example comes from a Mediaeval Nubian tombstone. The royal burial inscription from Soba East, capital of the Kingdom of Alwa, reads as follows: 'O God of the spirits and all flesh, Thou who hast rendered death ineffectual and has trodden down Hades, and hast given life to the world, rest the soul of (Thy) servant David, the King, in the bosom of Abraham and Isaac and Jacob, in a place of light, in a place of verdure, in a place of refreshment, whence pain and grief and mourning hath fled … The years from his birth when he was not a king (were) [..] whereas he was king 16 years 3 months. After the Martyrs 732 he completed (his life) in the month of Hathor the 2nd; Thursday.'

The Month of Hathor is a concept associated with the Ancient Egyptians. The fact that this appears on a Mediaeval Nubian tombstone may indicate that the Mediaeval Nubians inherited the Ancient Egyptian calendar. This also suggests that they inherited at least portions of the Ancient Egyptian astronomical lore.

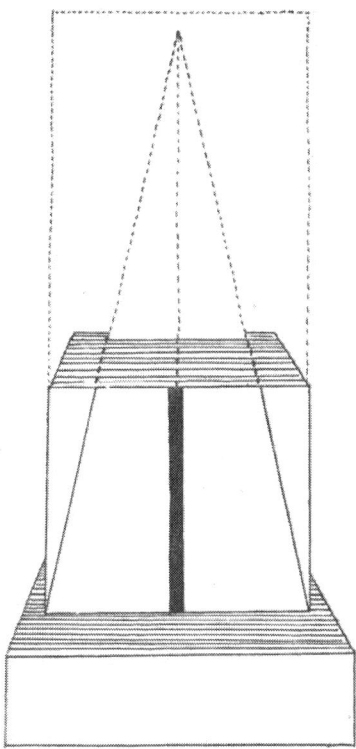

Figure 12. Instrument from the Kushite city of Meroë that enabled the tracking of the sun at the meridian. From Cheikh Anta Diop, *Precolonial Black Africa,* US, Lawrence Hill Books, 1987, p.198.

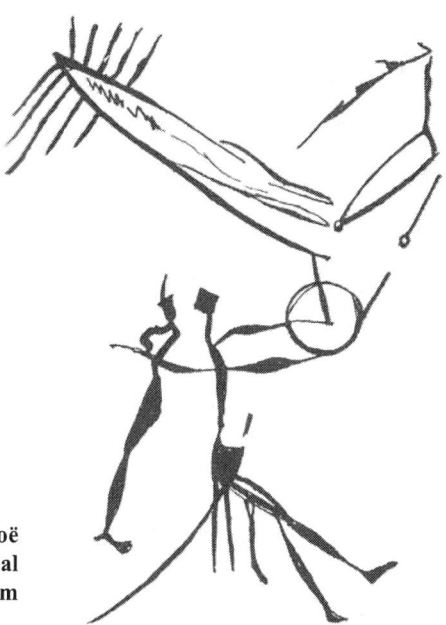

Figure 13. Petroglyph from Meroë showing people operating an astronomical instrument. Is this an astrolabe? From ibid., p.197.

Ethiopia

Information on early Ethiopian astronomy comes from two sets of source information. Some of the Ethiopian manuscripts contain astronomical texts that are related to the *Book of Enoch*. Other manuscripts contain tables and formulae to enable the calculation of Christian festivals such as Easter. Professor Otto Neugebauer made a special study of these documents. The manuscripts dated from the fourteenth to the nineteenth centuries. Since they were copies of older manuscripts Neugebauer could not give solid dates to the originals. There was one clear exception to this. Neugebauer explains: 'It is, however, a singularly fortunate accident that we have an Ethiopic table that can be dated to the years Diocletian 27 to 85 (A. D. 311 to 369).'

The manuscripts show that the Ethiopians freely drew upon astronomical ideas and concepts from the Coptic Egyptians, Greeks and Arabs. Some manuscripts show basic knowledge of the five planets (Mercury, Venus, Mars, Saturn and Jupiter). Some of these have diagrams of planetary periods. Others describe the 28 lunar mansions and include diagrams. However some of these manuscripts contain misunderstandings of these concepts too. They did not use the mansions to tell the time at night as was done in Timbuktu. Other manuscripts show the 12 signs or towers of the Zodiac, some also with diagrams. The Ethiopians combined the 12 gates from the *Book of Enoch* with the Zodiacal signs from Arabic and Latin sources. Some manuscripts describe lunar phases and lunar illumination, again some with diagrams. Other manuscripts mention solar eclipses in 1241 AD, 1528 and 1727. A manuscript mentions a lunar eclipse in 1620. An Ethiopian (and also a Chinese) manuscript recorded the appearance of a nova in 1618.

Thus the Ethiopians calculated a 354 day lunar year, a 364 day Enoch year, and a 365 day solar year with the 366 day leap year. What the Ethiopians never did, however, was to synthesize the different material (Coptic, Greek and Arabic) into a single coherent body of astronomy. Professor Neugebauer is also scathing about the fact that Ethiopia never advanced astronomy beyond the arithmetic necessary to maintain the Christian and Jewish calendars.

The Ethiopians drew up 532 year tables which combined much of these calculations for their religious calendars. However, Professor Neugebauer conceded that: 'the practical arrangement of the tables which had to provide the user with the dates both of Passover and of Easter and of the associated feast days shows real skill and understanding of the arithmetic structure of the relevant numerical sequences.'

However Professor Neugebauer cited one example from an Amharic manuscript which must have been original to the Ethiopian scribe who wrote it since 'the value for the lunar month ... is not known to me [i.e. Neugebauer] from any published source.' The manuscript gave the mean value of a synodic month as 29:31,50,7,57,30d. This is a base 60 division of a mean lunar month into $29 + 31/60 + 50/60^2 + 7/60^3 + 57/60^4 + 30/60^5$ days. This is a brilliant estimate. It is as good as the figure given by Wikipedia (i.e. 29 days, 12 hours, 44 minutes and 2.8 seconds).

Early Kenya

Other substantial research into East African astronomy came from the pen of two archaeologists working in Kenya in the 1970s who discovered a significant early site. Called Namoratunga II, Lynch and Robbins wrote a paper on it entitled: *Namoratunga: The First Archaeoastronomical Evidence in Sub-Saharan Africa,* 1978. The site was dated at 300 BC and is regarded as evidence of early astronomy in the Lake Turkana region of Kenya.

Nineteen pillars were found at the site. They were at all angles and were found to have been allied to certain stars. The archaeologists numbered the

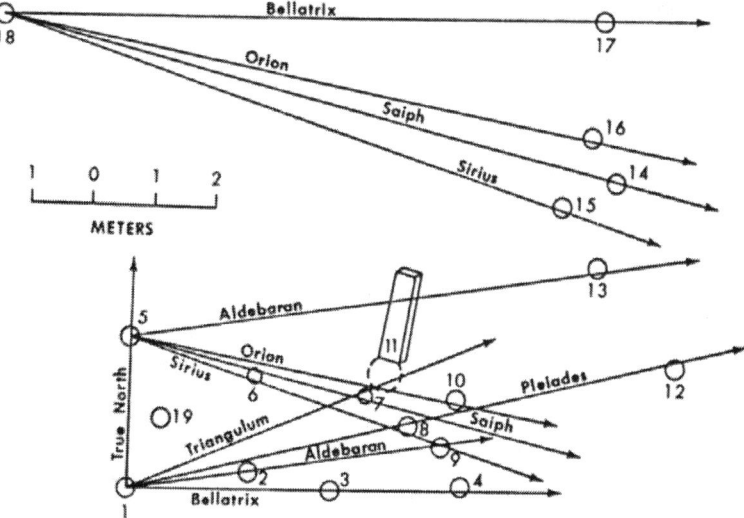

Figure 14. Pillar alignments at Namoratunga II in Kenya. *c.*300 BC.

pillars and suggested that their pillars 1, 5 and 18 were the sighting points. If they were correct in this assertion they concluded that from pillar one, the ancient astronomers were observing Triangulum, the Pleiades, Aldebaran and Bellatrix. From pillar five, the ancient astronomers were observing Aldebaran, Central Orion, Saiph and Sirius. From pillar 18, the ancient astronomers were observing Bellatrix, Central Orion, Saiph and Sirius.

Lynch and Robbins suggested that the ancient astronomers were observing the stars to create an accurate 354 day lunar year divided into 12 months. The idea was that the early astronomers waited for certain stars to line up against certain pillars in conjunction with the new moon. For the first month of the year, they waited for the star Triangulum. For the second month it was the Pleiades. For the third month it was Aldebaran, followed by Bellatrix, followed by Central Orion, followed by Saiph, followed by Sirius. For months eight, nine, ten, eleven and twelve, the astronomers observed the star Triangulum, but calculated it against the declining phases of the moon. This lunar calendar was one of the most accurate of the pre-Christian era calendars.

Great Zimbabwe

Concerning Great Zimbabwe, Professors Oliver and Fagan have pointed out that the New Moon ceremonies in May signalled the beginning of their civil calendar. Laurance Doyle, author of an encyclopaedia of the history of science, technology and medicine in the non-Western world has interesting things to say about the astronomical ideas encoded into the building of the Great Zimbabwe.

'[P]reliminary investigations do reveal that the native African peoples that built Great Zimbabwe were aware of the sky and may indeed have marked important astronomical seasonal events. For example, in a preliminary survey, a "chevron" pattern on the southeast corner of the large outer wall is bisected by the rising position of the Sun on the summer solstice from inside the enclosure, and aligns with what has been called the "altar" as well as an original pillar inside the enclosure. As this large patterning does not appear at any other place on the outer wall it would appear to be a conspicuous candidate for a summer solstice marker built into the Great Enclosure. In addition, a large passageway within the Great Enclosure--about 2 meters in width, 30 or so meters in (curving) length, with 10 meter high brick walls on either side, would allow a limited view of the sky with an angular extent and curvature matching the position and angular extent of the Milky Way overhead on the summer solstice. While the Milky Way was a very important calendrical marker for the Karanga people of this area [who are a part of the Shona] (Sicard 1969, McKosh 1979) this observation too must be confirmed with further research. Finally, from a cleared platform at the top of the Hill Complex, two large stones (approximately 5 meters in height) in close proximity to each other can be seen to form a slit directed precisely east which could have served as a solar marker for the equinoxes.'

Doyle does, however, stress that further scholarly verification is required before a definitive conclusion can be made: 'These and other observations are, however, preliminary and a better understanding of the calendrical systems of the early inhabitants of this region would substantially improve further investigations into any astronomical features that may have been built into the ruins at Great Zimbabwe.'

CHAPTER 5: MEDICINE AND SURGERY

Introduction

Professor Charles Finch wrote a classic essay on early African medicine and surgery entitled *The African Background to the Medical Science.* In this splendid 1983 essay, he gave startling examples of early East African medicine and surgery.

Kush and Nubia

In 1980, a scholar published a paper called *Tetracycline-Labeled Bone from Ancient Sudanese Nubia.* The paper appeared in *Science* magazine. The main finding was the discovery that early Mediaeval Nubian skeletons from 350 to 550 AD were found to have had tetracycline in their bones. However, the author of the paper did not know why this was the case.

Professor Finch, by contrast, drew the conclusion from the same evidence that the tetracyclene was used in such a quantity that suggested that its use was deliberate and pharmaceutical. Tetracycline is an antibiotic which derives from a mould belonging to the streptomyces family.

Later research, however, has found that the use of tetracycline in this region dated back to an even earlier period. Its use could be traced back to Kushite times.

Kenya, Tanzania and Uganda

Professor Finch points out that surgery in East Africa was traditionally at a high level. Traditional surgeons among the Massai of Kenya and Tanzania performed limb amputations and devised prostheses for severed limbs.

Some interesting information has survived about the 19th-century Kingdom of Banyoro in what is today known as Uganda. Medical practitioners in this kingdom routinely carried out autopsies on patients dying of unknown causes. A British medical doctor in 1879 witnessed an event that was quite extraordinary--a Caesarean section. In Europe Caesarean sections performed at the time had a 100% death rate for the

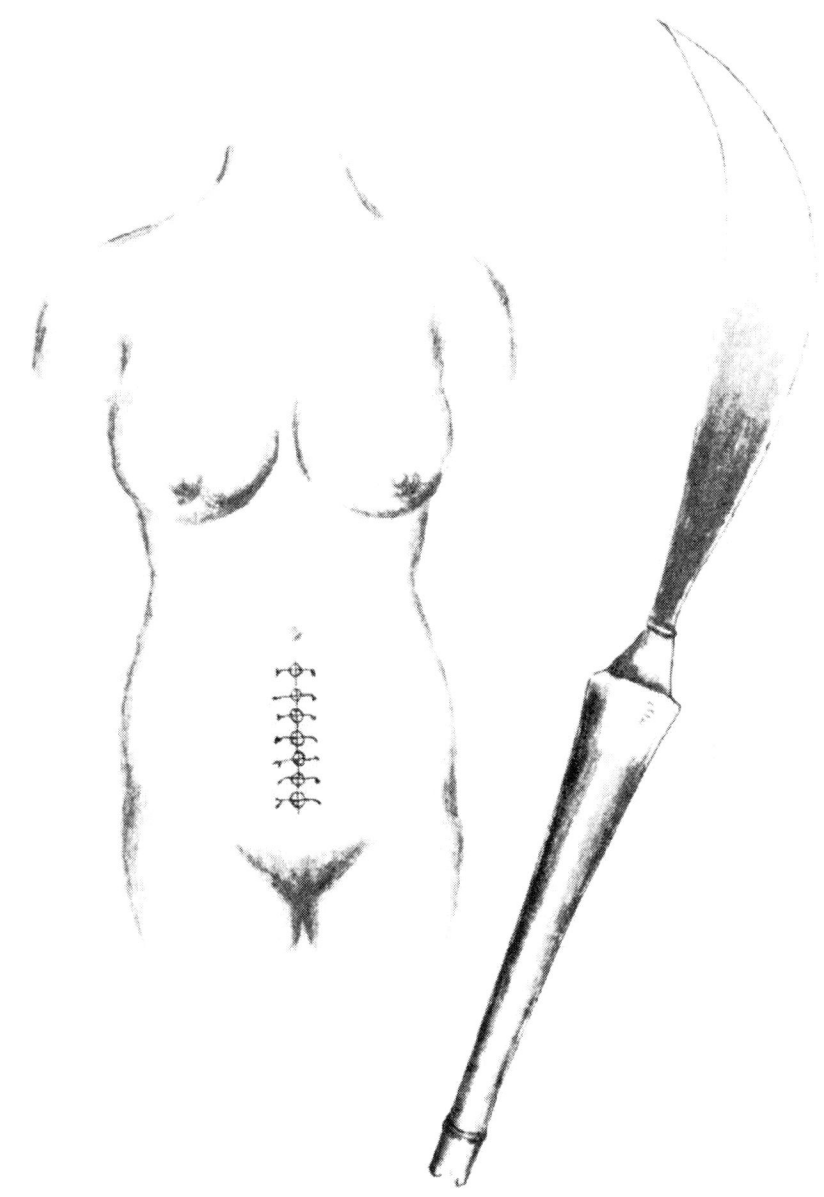

Figure 15. Knife and post caesarean wound derived from Dr R. W. Felkin's description, drawn by Sylvia Bakos.

mother. Dr R. W. Felkin witnessed a surgeon in Banyoro accompanied by two assistants carrying out a Caesarean section. The surgeon used anaesthetics, antiseptics, effective surgical techniques, and the sparing use of cautery iron to reduce bleeding. When Felkin left the kingdom to return home ten days later, both mother and baby were doing well. A few years later, Felkin wrote up what he witnessed in Uganda and his article appeared in an 1884 edition of the *Edinburgh Medical Journal.*

Other than the Finch essay, two splendid works have shed greater light on African medicine and surgery. Professor Richard Pankhurst wrote the splendid *An Introduction to the Medical History of Ethiopia.* Published in 1990, the book documented the medical and surgical practices of early Ethiopia and Somalia. Dr A. T. Bryant compiled the exquisite *Zulu Medicine and Medicine-Men* over many years in the late nineteenth and early twentieth centuries. Finally published in 1966 and 1983, the book drew many radical conclusions. For example, according to Dr Bryant: 'It is by no means an exaggeration to affirm that comparatively the average Zulu can boast of a larger share of pure scientific knowledge than the average European.'

Ethiopia

Ethiopia possesses a small but important number of medical manuscripts. Written in Ge'ez and Amharic, these texts date from the second half of the eighteenth century. Others were from the nineteenth and early twentieth centuries. Broad in nature, the texts cover illnesses, diseases and their treatments. They also cover and combine issues of a magical nature such as averting the evil eye, overcoming evil spirits, defeating your enemies, etcetera.

The scientific content of these texts describe treatments for epilepsy, fever, syphilis, rabies, skin diseases, kidney problems, haemorrhoids, constipation, diarrhoea, dysuria, itching, coughing, sterility and even snoring. The texts describe thousands of prescriptions that involved an extensive pharmacopeia derived from the vegetable, animal and mineral kingdoms.

Visitors to Ethiopia from the seventeenth to the nineteenth centuries reported how the Ethiopians controlled the spread of epidemics like smallpox, cholera, typhus and influenza. They retired to the mountainous areas at the first evidence of an outbreak of disease. They prevented the movement of people to and from affected areas. They prevented the movement of cattle in the case of cattle diseases. They even burned the sick alive in their houses in extreme cases.

Visitors also describe how the Ethiopians used counterirritation by burning as a medical technique. One visitor described it as 'very efficacious.' They treated inflammation of the lungs by making small burns on the chest. They also treated rheumatism using similar techniques.

Another technique frequently used was cautery. They used it to disinfect skin. It was used to prevent bleeding and also used in the treatment of scorpion bites, snake bites and bites from other creatures.

The Ethiopians successfully practised the inoculation of populations against smallpox. They attempted similar inoculation techniques for the treatment of rabies and syphilis. They combined the attempted inoculation techniques with a range of other treatments.

In the case of rabies, Ethiopian manuscripts from the eighteenth century specifically mention that a bite from a rabid dog was often fatal. It was thus a serious condition requiring urgent attention. Nineteenth century manuscripts show that the Ethiopians were aware that the incubation period for rabies was 40 days. After carefully cleaning and disinfecting the wound, they treated rabies by using a range of purgatives. Purgatives were prescriptions designed to deliberately induce vomiting or diarrhoea in the patient.

In the case of syphilis, the Ethiopians traditionally prescribed a range of purgatives but also taenicides. Taenicides were prescriptions that killed tapeworms in the stomach which was also supposed to help in combating syphilis. *Ximenia americana* was rated highly by the Ethiopians as a topical treatment for syphilitic sores. Sometimes the prescriptions were combined with bathing in thermal springs. With temperatures of between 49 and 60 degrees Celsius, naturally occurring thermal springs were also thought to be efficacious in the treatment of rheumatism, arthritis, skin diseases, wounds and leprosy.

Ethiopians living near the Sudanese border consumed mercury rich earth with water or applied it topically to treat syphilis. The efficacy of mercury in the treatment of syphilis has been noted around the world. In Gondar vapour baths were established. These were specially constructed stone buildings that were kept very hot. The syphilitic patient stayed in this hot environment and was prescribed sarsaparilla or mercury--treatments also in use in Europe nearly a hundred years earlier.

Surgery was practised extensively and covered simple and complex operations. A nineteenth century visitor wrote that they 'excelled in surgery' and displayed 'truly amazing' skill and courage. They extracted tonsils. They even opened the stomach, took out intestines, cleaned them and replaced them in the stomach. They routinely carried out amputations that involved cutting the skin and the tendons, followed by the ligaments. The wound was covered by powders, cinders or leaves. Alternatively, they were cauterised using hot irons. Surgeons in Tegré performed Caesarean sections for difficult childbirths.

Bone setting was practised and with a high degree of success. Splints were made of bone or wood. In Harar they made plates of iron, lead or copper. Fractured skulls were often treated by replacing damaged parts of a skull by bones from goats or sheep.

Somalia

According to Professor Richard Pankhurst, Somali traditional medicine and surgery shared some features with the Ethiopian. They used counterriritation almost as a panacea. They used fumigation in the treating of ill patients by covering them with hot sand and placing aromatics under their bed. They used purgatives and also sulphur to treat syphilis. Most importantly, they were excellent bone setters. They set fractures by supporting them with twigs and reeds woven together. They were even able to insert bones from sheep into humans.

Zulu

According to Dr A. T. Bryant, most traditional medical practitioners among the Zulu followed their fathers into the profession. Initially, the sons worked as their father's assistants. They worked as his messengers, herb gathers, and general helpers. They accompanied their fathers on his excursions as a medicine-bearer, picking up by instruction and observation, medical knowledge and skills. After many years as an assistant, the young man might strike out by himself and establish his own practice. He typically shared remedies with neighbouring doctors and grew in knowledge and expertise through the practice of consulting. After twenty years or more, he learned all there was to learn about the Zulu pharmacopeia and local pathology.

The medical practitioners were called *i-nyanga* in Zulu and *i-nyangi* in Xhosa. Their knowledge and practice covered medicine but also overlapped with the arts associated with priests and diviners. In Zulu society, however, there was a distinction between the *i-nyanga yokwelapha* (the doctor for curing) and the *i-nyanga yokubhula* (the doctor for divining).

Dr Bryant was scornful about the poor state of Zulu knowledge of human anatomy and physiology. Knowledge of the nervous system seemed close to nil. However the Zulu doctors were conversant with symptoms and diseases. According to Dr Bryant, the key rule seems to have been that there were as many diseases as there were symptoms. This is not an entirely acceptable methodology, since the same condition could cause multiple symptoms! Amongst the drug therapies used were drastic astringents and, as elsewhere, drastic purgatives.

Dr Bryant documented the names of 225 plants used in Zulu medicine. Andrew Smith, another authority wrote on 150 plants used by the Xhosa and Fingo. Smith also mentions another 240 plants in Zulu medical use. In total there were around 700 plants used in Zulu medicine. In addition, the pharmacopeia covered a wide range from the mineral, vegetable and animal kingdoms, terrestrial and marine.

Dr Bryant says: 'In spite of such blind empiricism it cannot be denied that the native doctor does sometimes work a cure, sometimes quite a startling cure, where the efforts of European physicians have proved utterly unavailing. Remedies he has ... without number, and some of them truly helpful, suited to every ill--physical, mental, moral and social--that man is heir to. Frequently it is to these we may attribute his success.'

However, some of the other successes were based on the placebo effect. In the opinion of Dr Bryant, 'many ... cures, and, it may be added, of many ... ailments, is not the action of matter on matter, of drug on flesh, but in those occult regions where mind works on mind and mind on flesh.'

According to Dr Bryant, the traditional Zulu methods of preparing medicines 'are much like our own.' Medicines were given as cold infusions that combined cold water with the chopped or powdered medicine. Some were given as hot infusions prepared like tea. Others were decoctions that were simmered. Some were given as powders. Some medicines were applied topically as liquids, ointments, lotions, and powders. As elsewhere, the Zulus had vapour and sweating baths. Finally, the Zulus practiced blood-letting, an idea widely practised in many countries, even in Europe.

The Zulu doctors had treatments for a wide range of ailments. Dr Bryant details the plant materials used in the treatment of broken limbs and sprains, catarrh, chest pains, chronic coughing, dropsy, dry cough, earache, eczema, expectoration of blood, extraction of thorns, febrile complaints, gangrenous rectitis, gonorrhoea, headache, heartburn, heart complaints, impotence, indigestion, infantile thrush, intercostal neuralgia, intestinal parasites, kidney disease, measles, nausea, ophthalmia, paralysis, piles, pleurisy, rheumatism, scrofula, skin sores, smallpox, snake bites, spinal disease, stomach and intestinal complaints, syphilis, tapeworm, toothache, urinary complaints, and wounds.

They also had treatments for 'barrenness', 'insanity' and 'hysteria.' Less controversially, they also had prescriptions that produced a hair dye. They also had a vermin killer.

In summary, Bryant found that some of the traditional Zulu medicines and medical procedures were worthless and even dangerous. On the other hand, he found that Zulu doctors were familiar 'with certain curative herbs and plants long before the Western medical world learned about these.'

CHAPTER 6: SHIPPING AND NAVIGATION

Ethiopia

Axum at the height of its power was an important naval force. Controlling the Straits of Bab-al-Mandeb, they dominated one of the three main shipping highways in the ancient world.

Axum itself had two famous ports Azab and Adule (also known as Adulis). Their merchant vessels were so famous that a Mesopotamian poet used them to describe the progress of royal caravan. According to him, it forged ahead like one of the ships of Adulis whose 'prow cuts through the foam of the water as a gambler divides the dust with his hand.' Axumite ships moved goods to and from Egypt, the Roman provinces, the Mediterranean, Arabia, India, Sri-Lanka and China.

East African Coast

East African ships were on the Indian Ocean. The East African vessels with sails were called *mtepe* and those with sales and oars were called *dua la mtepe*. Some of the ships reached 70 tonnes in weight. One such example is a model in the Fort Jesus Museum of Mombasa. The antiquity of these ships are deserving of notice. Dating from at least the first century AD, the ships appear in the famous Greek guidebook to the seas, *The Periplus of the Eritrean Sea*. The *Periplus* mentions that the East Africans made 'sewn boats.' This fact is important because many scholars including the learned Professor Charles Finch incorrectly state that these ships were of Arabian origin.

Dr Basil Davidson, the great English Africanist, says: 'The sailing rig in use today has changed very little since the great trading days of the past. East African sailors were attacking their ships against the wind, up to an angle of 35 degrees, long before Europeans had learned the necessary technique. The Africans who manned, and still man these vessels, are the Swahili ...'

East African mariners used the monsoon winds to sail to and from Asia. In April the south-west monsoon starts. By around June or July it created a

Figure 16. Model of an East African *mtepe* and other Swahili craft in the Fort Jesus Museum in Mombasa, Kenya. (Photo: Robin Walker.)

strong northerly current that flows up the Somali coast towards India. The African mariners would set sail at this point. The sailors would typically stay in the Asian ports for several months waiting for their return journey. To return to Africa, the East African mariners would wait for the north-east monsoon which blew from India and the Persian Gulf toward East Africa and down its coastline. The monsoon began in November but the mariners would actually set sail when the monsoon reached its full strength in January.

The East Africans sailed at least as far as Java, selling their ivory and steel. One interesting question was: Did they sail any further?

In 1414 the Sultan of Malindi, in what is now Kenya, sent the Chinese emperor a giraffe. The strange beast caused a sensation at the Imperial Court but the most important fact as far as I am concerned is that the distance represented by the journey is twice as far as the journey that the Malians undertook in 1311 from West Africa to Panama.

However, on 14 September 2013, *The Sydney Morning Herald,* an Australian newspaper, published an explosive article entitled *Out of Africa.* The subtitle to the article asks: *'How did medieval coins from East Africa end up on a remote island off the Northern Territory?'* Moreover: *'It's a mystery that may rewrite Australia's early history.'*

Coins that originated in the Swahili city state of Kilwa were found on an island off Australia's Northern Territory. They date back about 1000 years. This therefore raises questions about how they got there. The article mentions a comment from a scholar researching this question, Tim Stone. He said: "If there are Kilwa coins there from 1000 years ago, the simplest explanation to me is that there were Kilwans there 1000 years ago." Moreover: "To me, that makes much more sense than somebody carrying them together and losing them in one spot."

If Stone is correct, this suggests that East African seafarers even got as far as Northern Australia, one thousand years ago!

CONCLUSION

The study of East African science and technology is pretty much in its infancy. While 900 documents survive dating from the Kushite period written in the ancient Meroitic script, these documents cannot yet be read by scholars today.

Thousands of documents from Mediaeval Nubia have survived from Qasr Ibrim in eight different languages. These are, however, ecclesiastical documents. I do not yet know the scientific and technological content of these documents.

Similarly, a quarter of a million manuscripts have survived in Ethiopia. One of them, the *Gospels of Abba Garima,* has recently been found to date from before 650 AD. It is thus believed to be the oldest illuminated Christian manuscript in the world. We know of the astronomical, mathematical and medical data of these manuscripts, but what else is in them?

It is known that the Ethiopian city of Harar and many of the Swahili cities were centres of Islamic instruction. Did any of these places create a university culture to equal Timbuktu, Djenné and Walata? I am not yet in a position to answer this question.

Professor Albert Churchward writing in 1910 mentions evidence that one of the southern African ruins contained manuscripts covered with writing. He said that a White South African burned many of these manuscripts but many still remained there. What happened to these manuscripts? What was in them? Again, I am not yet in a position to answer these questions.

SOURCES OF INFORMATION

Introduction

David Okuefuna (Executive Producer), *Go Forth and Multiply*, UK, The Open University for BBC 4, Television Programme, 2005

Chapter 1: Mathematics

Paulus Gerdes, *Geometry From Africa*, US, The Mathematical Association of America, 1999, pp.89-125

Otto Neugebauer, *Ethiopic Astronomy and Computus*, Germany, Osterreiche Akademie Der Wissenschaften, 1979, pp.7-10, 13-18, 27-66, 132, 175-177, 221-222

Chapter 2: Architecture

J. Theodore Bent, *The Ruined Cities of Mashonaland*, 3rd Edition, UK, Longmans, Green, and Co., 1902, pp.110-1

Charles Bonnet, *The Kingdom of Kerma*, in *Sudan: Ancient Kingdoms of the Nile*, edited by Dietrich Wildung, France, The Institut du monde arabe, 1997, pp.89-90

John Lewis Burckhardt, *Travels in Nubia*, UK, John Murray, 1819, p.500

Camerapix, *Ethiopia: A Tourist Paradise*, Ethiopia, Ethiopian Tourist Commission, 1996, whole book

Vivian Davies and Renée Friedman, *Egypt*, UK, British Museum Press, 1998, pp.103-7, 122-9

João de Barros, *Mines and Fortresses*, in *African Civilization Revisited*, edited by Basil Davidson, US, Africa World Press, 1991, p.182

H. N. Chittick, *A Guide to the Ruins of Kilwa,* Tanzania, Ministry of Community Development and Culture, 1965, whole booklet

Basil Davidson, *A Guide to African History,* US, Zenith Books, 1965, pp.30-32

Cheikh Anta Diop, *Precolonial Black Africa,* US, Lawrence Hill Books, 1987, pp.196-197

David Dugan, *Time Life's Lost Civilizations,* video series, *Africa, A History Denied,* Holland, Time Life Video, 1995

Nnamdi Elleh, *African Architecture: Evolution and Transformation,* US, McGraw-Hill, 1997, pp.44-46, 133-137, 149, 165-166 and 209-214

Charles Finch, *The Star of Deep Beginnings,* US, Khenti, 1998, pp.142-160

Peter Garlake, *Early Art and Architecture of Africa,* UK, Oxford University Press, 2002, pp.54-63, 67-68, 75-84, 88-92, 171-184

Graham Hancock, *The Beauty of Historic Ethiopia,* Kenya, Camerapix, 1996, whole book

S. Jakobielski, *Christian Nubia at the height of its civilization,* in *UNESCO General History of Africa: Volume III,* ed M. Al Fasi, UK, Heinemann, 1988, pp.200-204

Ronald Lewcock, *Zanj, the East African Coast,* in *Shelter in Africa,* ed Paul Oliver, UK, Barrie & Jenkins, 1971, pp.80-87

Geoffrey S. Mileham, *Churches in Lower Nubia,* US, University of Philadelphia, 1910, whole book

Roland Oliver and Brian M. Fagan, *Africa in the Iron Age,* UK, Cambridge University Press, 1975, p.125

P. L. Shinnie and M. Shinnie, *New Light on Medieval Nubia,* in *Papers in African Prehistory,* ed J. D. Fage and R. A. Oliver, UK, Cambridge University Press, 1970, pp.283-284

F. M. C. Stokes, *Zimbabwe,* in *The Geographical Magazine, Volume II: No.2,* edited by Michael Huxley, UK, The Geographical Magazine, December 1935, pp. 143-153

Derek A. Welsby, *The Medieval Kingdoms of Nubia,* UK, The British Museum Press, 2002, whole book

Dietrich Wildung, *Egypt from Prehistory to the Romans,* Germany, Taschen, 1997, pp.42-43, 180-189

Chancellor Williams, *The Destruction of Black Civilization,* US, Third World Press, 1987, pp.149-151

Chapter 3: Metallurgy

J. Theodore Bent, *The Ruined Cities of Mashonaland,* 3rd Edition, UK, Longmans, Green, and Co., 1902, p.308

Ian D. Colvin, *Zimbabwe's Ruins of Mystery,* in *Wonders of the Past, Volume 2,* ed Sir J. A. Hammerton, UK, Amalgamated Press, 1937, p.969

Charles Finch, *The Star of Deep Beginnings,* US, Khenti, 1998, pp.28, 30-32, 38-47, 50-51

Peter Garlake, *Early Art and Architecture of Africa,* UK, Oxford University Press, 2002, p.84

Peter Garlake, *The Kingdoms of Africa,* UK, Elsevier Phaidon, 1978, pp.78-79

A. A. Hakem, *The civilization of Napata and Meroe,* in *UNESCO, General History of Africa, Volume II,* edited by G. Mokhtar, UK, James Currey, 1990, p.311

Roland Oliver and Brian Fagan, *Africa in the Iron Age,* UK, Cambridge University Press, 1975, p.109.

Debra Shore, *Steel-Making in Ancient Africa,* in *Blacks in Science: Ancient and Modern,* edited by Ivan Van Sertima, US, Transaction Publishers, 1983, pp.157-162

Dietrich Wildung, *The Treasure of Amanishakheto,* in *Sudan: Ancient Kingdoms of the Nile,* edited by Dietrich Wildung, France, The Institut du monde arabe, 1997, pp.301-340.

Chapter 4: Astronomy

Cheikh Anta Diop, *Precolonial Black Africa,* US, Lawrence Hill Books, 1987, pp.196-198

Laurance R. Doyle, *Astronomy of Africa,* in *Encyclopaedia of the History of Science, Technology and Medicine in Non-Western Cultures.* See internet at http://www.safaris.cc/8art.encyclo.htm.

Charles Finch, *The Star of Deep Beginnings,* US, Khenti, 1998, pp.168-169 and 195-198

Lady Lugard, *A Tropical Dependency,* UK, James Nisbet & Co., 1906, p.220

Otto Neugebauer, *Ethiopic Astronomy and Computus,* Germany, Osterreiche Akademie Der Wissenschaften, 1979, pp.7-8, 13-14, 18, 20, 91, 95, 99, 107-108, 183-184, 198, 200-201, 227, 232-233

Roland Oliver and Brian M. Fagan, *Africa in the Iron Age,* UK, Cambridge University Press, 1975, p.208

Ivan Van Sertima editor, *Blacks in Science: Ancient and Modern,* US, Transaction Publishers, 1983, pp.10 and 51-56

Derek A. Welsby, *The Medieval Kingdoms of Nubia,* UK, The British Museum Press, 2002, p.62

Chapter 5: Medicine and Surgery

A. T. Bryant, *Zulu Medicine and Medicine-Men,* South Africa, Centaur Publishers, 1966, pp. Inside cover note, 7, 10, 11, 13, 15-16, 19-20, 22-23, 86-115

Charles S. Finch, *The African Background of Medical Science* in *Blacks in Science: Ancient and Modern,* edited by Ivan Van Sertima, US, Transaction Publishers, 1983, pp.151-153 and 155

Charles S. Finch, *AFRICA and The Birth of Science and Technology: A Brief Overview,* US, Khenti, 1992, pp.25-26, 29-32 and 39

Richard Pankhurst, *An Introduction to the Medical History of Ethiopia,* US, Red Sea Press, 1990, pp.26-30, 75-80, 93-101, 104-111, 113-136

Chapter 6: Shipping and Navigation

Lisa Clausen, *Out of Africa,* in *The Sydney Morning Herald,* Australia, 14 September 2013. See internet at http://www.smh.com.au/national/out-of-africa-20130909-2tes7.html

Basil Davidson, *African Kingdoms,* Netherlands, Time-Life Books, 1967, p.42

Basil Davidson, *Africa,* television series part 3: *Caravans of Gold,* UK, Michael Beazley, Rm Arts, Channel Four Television & Nigerian Television, 1984

David Dugan, *Time Life's Lost Civilizations,* video series, *Africa, A History Denied,* Holland, Time Life Video, 1995.

Charles S. Finch, *The Star of Deep Beginnings,* US, Khenti, 1998, pp.220-221

Ivan Van Sertima, *Early America Revisited,* US, Transaction Publishers, 1992, p.17

Conclusion

Martin Bailey, *Discovery of earliest illuminated manuscript,* in *The Art Newspaper, No.214,* June 2010. See internet at http://ethiopianheritagefund.org/artsNewspaper.html

Albert Churchward, *The Signs and Symbols of Primordial Man,* UK, George Allen & Co., 1910, p.75

Derek A. Welsby, *The Medieval Kingdoms of Nubia,* UK, The British Museum Press, 2002, p.241

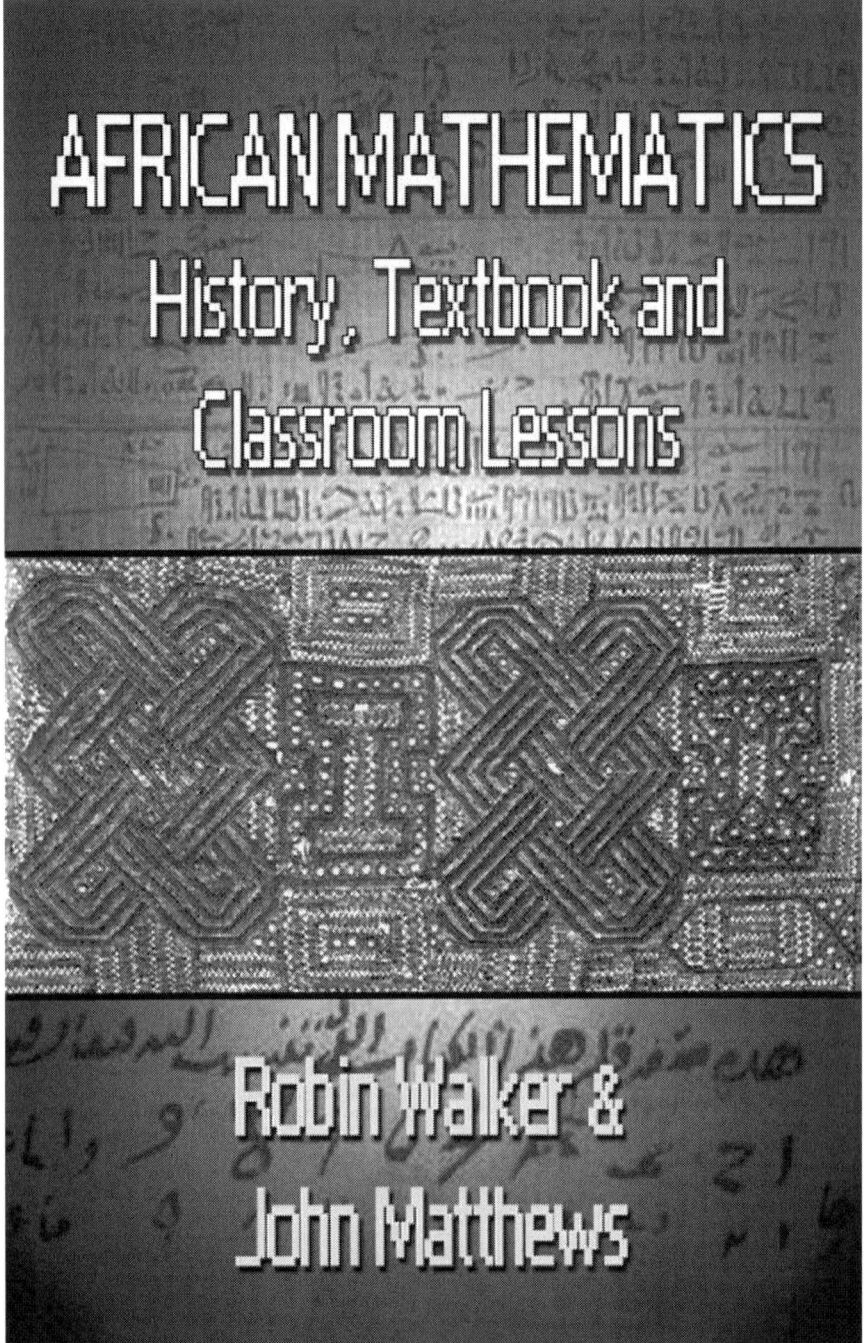

AFRICAN MATHEMATICS
History, Textbook and
Classroom Lessons

Robin Walker &
John Matthews

Also available.

PART FOUR

THE AUTHOR

ROBIN WALKER

Biography

Robin Walker 'The Black History Man' was born in London but has also lived in Jamaica. He attended the London School of Economics and Political Science where he read Economics.

In 1991 and 1992, he studied African World Studies with the brilliant Dr Femi Biko and later with Mr Kenny Bakie. Between 1993 and 1994, he trained as a secondary school teacher at Edge Hill College (linked to the University of Lancaster).

Since 1992 and up to the present period, Robin Walker has lectured in adult education, taught university short courses, and chaired conferences in African World Studies, Egyptology and Black History. The venues have been in Toxteth (Liverpool), Manchester, Leeds, Bradford, Huddersfield, Birmingham, Cambridge, Buckinghamshire and London.

Since 1994 he has taught Economics, Business & Finance, Mathematics, Information Communications Technology, PSHE/Citizenship and also History at various schools in London and Essex.

In 1999 he wrote *Classical Splendour: Roots of Black History* published in the UK by Bogle L'Ouverture Publications. In the same year, he co-authored (with Siaf Millar) *The West African Empire of Songhai,* a textbook used by many schools across the country.

In 2000 he co-authored (again with Siaf Millar) *Sword, Seal and Koran,* another book on the Songhai Empire of West Africa.

In 2006 he wrote the seminal *When We Ruled.* This was the most advanced synthesis on Ancient and Mediaeval African history ever written by a single author. It was a massive expansion of his earlier book *Classical Splendour: Roots of Black History* and established his reputation as the leading Black History educational service provider.

In 2008 he wrote *Before The Slave Trade,* a highly pictorial companion volume to *When We Ruled.*

Between 2011 and 2013 he wrote a series of e-books for download sold through Amazon Kindle.

In 2013 he co-authored (with Siaf Millar and Saran Keita) *Everyday Life In An Early West African Empire*. It was a massive expansion on the earlier book *Sword, Seal & Koran*. He updated *When We Ruled* by incorporating nearly all the images from *Before The Slave Trade*. He also wrote a trilogy of science books entitled *Blacks and Science Volumes One, Two* and *Three*.

In 2014 he wrote *The Rise and Fall of Black Wall $treet and the Seven Key Empowerment Principles, Blacks and Religion Volume One* and *If you want to learn Early African History START HERE*. He also co-authored (with John Matthews) *African Mathematics: History, Textbook and Classroom Lessons*.

In 2015 he wrote *19 Lessons in Black History* and *The Black Musical Tradition and Early Black Literature*. He also wrote *Blacks and Religion Volume Two*.

Speaking Engagements

Looking for a speaker for your next event?

The author Robin Walker 'The Black History Man' is dynamic and engaging, both as a speaker and a workshop leader. He brings Black or African history alive, making it relevant for the present generation. You will love his perfect blend of accessibility, engagement, and academic rigour where learning becomes fun.

Walker is available to give speaking engagements to a variety of audiences.

Motivational crowds, general audiences, schools and parents will enjoy Walker's highly engaging presentation *Sub Saharan Africa in the Mainstream of Science History*.

To book Robin Walker for your next event, send an email to historicalwalker@yahoo.com

Short Courses by Robin Walker

Would you like to deepen your learning in history and the history of science by studying with Robin Walker?

As part of his mission to get adults to engage with Black history, Robin Walker 'The Black History Man,' is offering you the chance to learn more about Black or African contributions to history.

For this reason, The Black History Man is teaching a short course entitled *Black people in the History of Science and Technology.* The programme consists of six content laden seminars:

1. Ancient Egyptian Contributions to Science and Technology
2. The Mysterious Sciences of the Great Pyramid
3. West and Central African Contributions to Science and Technology
4. East and South African Contributions to Science and Technology
5. African American Pioneers of Invention
6. African American Pioneers of Science

For more details on this course or any other enquiries, send an email to historicalwalker@yahoo.com

142

Also available.

INDEX

20632092R00084

Printed in Great Britain
by Amazon